From I

To Aa...

D0406811

"Getting tech wise starts with downloading God's wisdom on what it means to be human. Andy gives families the tools they need to decide together who they want to be and how technology can help rather than hinder. If you aren't sure how to put technology in its 'proper place' in your home, Andy will guide you and challenge your thinking."

Mark Batterson, *New York Times* best-selling author of *The Circle Maker*; lead pastor, National Community Church

"To be honest, before I opened this book, I expected to be challenged on the topic of screen time for my kids. I was, certainly. What I did not expect was to be offered a vision for family life and faith and character so compelling and inspiring that it made me weep, made me reconsider many aspects of our home, made me profoundly thankful for this beautiful and important book. I'll give away a case, at least."

Shauna Niequist, *New York Times* best-selling author of *Present over Perfect* and *Bread & Wine*

"Every day my husband and I face questions about how to handle technology with our three kids. No parent today can leave their kids to their own devices (pun intended). Andy's message and model have strengthened our commitment to use technology to unite—and not divide—our family."

Kara Powell, executive director, Fuller Youth Institute; coauthor of *Growing Young*

"I don't know many people who can prophetically speak into culture with more freshness and certain insight than Andy Crouch. His voice is a gift to the church and is needed more than ever right now. As a new parent who is asking all kinds of questions about raising kids in today's technological world, I couldn't have found this resource at a better time."

Jefferson Bethke, *New York Times* best-selling author of *Jesus > Religion* and *It's Not What You Think*

"In a tech-wise world, 'tech' is a lot easier to come by than 'wise.' Andy Crouch has written a humane, deeply thoughtful book that will be a blessing in the best sense of that grand old word."

John Ortberg, senior pastor, Menlo Church; author of *All The Places to Go . . . How Will You Know?*

"If your family's devices and gadgets seem to have staged a hostile takeover in your home, Andy Crouch can help. With winsome humor and down-to-earth advice, Andy will show you how to nurture a thriving home life through a wise and balanced use of technology."

Jim Daly, president, Focus on the Family

"We have never done this before: the human race has never parented with tech devices in every corner of our homes. For parents who battle the screen time, the password management, the filtering, and the begging, we finally have the book we've been waiting for. *The Tech-Wise Family* offers practical, positive approaches for parents to manage technology in the family and the biblical framework for why those approaches are appropriate and healthy. Modern parenting often feels like sprinting a marathon blindfolded, but voices like Andy Crouch's add light to our journey and remind us of our end goal. Read *The Tech-Wise Family*, implement the principles, and watch your family thrive as a result."

Alexandra Kuykendall, mother of four;
author of *Loving My Actual Life*;
cohostess of *The Open Door Sisterhood* podcast.

"Micro practices have macro implications for our lives. The rituals we adopt around the tiny computers in our pockets can either eat us alive or release us for relationship. *The Tech-Wise Family* is profoundly insightful and immediately practical. Crouch invites us into habits and rhythms in which technology serves our calling to be human and helps us to resist the temptation to serve the gods that glitter. It's a book I wish our family had read ten years ago."

James K. A. Smith, Calvin College; author of *You Are What You Love: The Spiritual Power of Habit*

"Families need this book. Churches need this book. I need this book. One of the most important questions of discipleship in this digital era is how we relate to our technologies. The habits formed now could have even more important implications for the yet-unseen future. Andy Crouch guides us with brilliance, wisdom, humility, and authority."

Russell Moore, president, The Ethics & Religious Liberty Commission of the Southern Baptist Convention; author of *Onward: Engaging Culture without Losing the Gospel*

"As parents of two young boys and pastors of a church with hundreds of millennials, we found ourselves repeatedly shouting 'Yes!' to Andy Crouch's call to unplug. In *The Tech-Wise Family* we are reminded that there is fullness of life beyond the encroachments of the cybernetic revolution."

Revs. Gabriel and Jeanette Salguero, cofounders, National Latino Evangelical Coalition; pastors, Calvario City Church

"*The Tech-Wise Family* is one of the most important things I've read this year. Most of us have a sinking feeling that our children (and ourselves!) have slipped into a technology haze. Andy's book has helped organize my thinking and provided practical ways to put boundaries around technology's influence. And as an educator, this book includes great lessons to ensure technology has a proper, meaningful role in our nation's classrooms."

Nicole Baker Fulgham, founder of The Expectations Project; author of *Educating All God's Children*

THE
TECH-WISE
FAMILY

THE
TECH-WISE
FAMILY

Everyday Steps for Putting Technology in Its Proper Place

ANDY CROUCH

With new insights and research from Barna

BakerBooks

a division of Baker Publishing Group
Grand Rapids, Michigan

Text © 2017 by Andy Crouch
Research © 2017 by Barna Group

Published by Baker Books
a division of Baker Publishing Group
PO Box 6287, Grand Rapids, MI 49516-6287
www.bakerbooks.com

Printed in the United States of America

Library of Congress Cataloging-in-Publication Data
Names: Crouch, Andy, author.
Title: The tech-wise family : everyday steps for putting technology in its proper
    place / Andy Crouch ; with new insights and research from Barna.
Description: Grand Rapids : Baker Books, 2017. | Includes bibliographical
    references.
Identifiers: LCCN 2016048801 | ISBN 9780801018664 (cloth)
Subjects: LCSH: Parenting—Religious aspects—Christianity. | Technology—
    Religious aspects—Christianity. | Families—Religious aspects—Christianity.
Classification: LCC BV4529 .C77 2017 | DDC 261.5/6—dc23
LC record available at https://lccn.loc.gov/2016048801

Unless otherwise noted, Scripture quotations are from the New Revised Standard
Version of the Bible, copyright © 1989, by the Division of Christian Education of
the National Council of the Churches of Christ in the United States of America.
Used by permission. All rights reserved.

Scripture quotations labeled NIV are from the Holy Bible, New International Ver-
sion®. NIV®. Copyright © 1973, 1978, 1984, 2011 by Biblica, Inc.™ Used by permission of Zondervan. All rights reserved worldwide. www.zondervan.com

Scripture quotations labeled NLT are from the *Holy Bible*, New Living Translation,
copyright © 1996, 2004, 2015 by Tyndale House Foundation.
Used by permission of Tyndale House Publishers, Inc., Carol
Stream, Illinois 60188. All rights reserved.

Andy Crouch is represented by Creative Trust, Inc., 210
Jamestown Park Drive, Suite 200, Brentwood, TN 37027,
www.creativetrust.com.

18 19 20 21 22 23   7 6

Contents

Foreword

AMY CROUCH

As the author's daughter, I've been living with tech-wise parenting for sixteen years. Some might say my older brother, who's had it for nineteen years, would be even better qualified to write this foreword. I, however, would argue that as test subject number two, I've enjoyed an even more refined approach. So if you are wondering how tech-wise parenting actually works out, I might be able to help you.

I think the best part of tech-wise parenting, for me, has been its focus on "something older and better than the newest thing." The key word is *better*. Tech-wise parenting isn't simply intended to eliminate technology but to put better things in its place. Technology promises that it can provide wonder. Take a picture with the proper filters and you'll be awestruck—it will look better than real life! But this promise is deceptive. My iPhone's wonder generators, from Instagram to Temple Run, turn out to be only distractions from the things that really spark wonder. Thanks to tech-wise parenting, I've discovered a world out there that is better than anything technology can offer—as close as our front lawn.

I'll be honest, though. If you're hoping that being tech wise will neatly eliminate technology's harmful influences from your children's lives, you're set up for disappointment. I haven't been totally able to escape its pitfalls. I probably have a healthier relationship with technology than some of my peers, but I still have problems—aimlessly scrolling through websites and apps even when I need to do important things (such as sleep, eat, do homework, or make cookies). And having a comparatively healthy relationship isn't much of an accomplishment, given what I'm comparing it to. I'll probably be figuring out how to balance technology and productivity through my whole adult life, and I doubt even the most tech-wise parenting could prevent that.

Tech-wise parenting has added wonder to my life, though, and that's enough. The real world is so fantastic that getting a taste of it makes even the most jaded kid want more. Not only have I always known that wonder is out there; I've been taught how to search for it. No multitude of glowing rectangles will ever be able to replace a single bumblebee. And that's the real legacy of tech-wise parenting for me. It has shown me where to look for what I need most. Wonder comes from opening your eyes wider, not bringing the screen closer.

If you're worrying that not having a TV will wreak havoc on your child's life, don't worry. Well, maybe it will wreak havoc, but it'll be the good kind. I did end up drawing on the bathroom wall with neon green crayons meant only for the tub, but I also learned to paint tiny watercolors (we still have them in the tiny boxes violin rosin comes in), wrote songs about cows in the car (Mom still has the recording), and came up with stories about umbrella-fencing matches (I thought that was a brilliant idea as a kid and still hope to sneak an umbrella-fencing scene into a movie someday).

OK, my parents' approach to parenting has caused a certain amount of havoc and even difficulty. But since that's not the best way to persuade you to buy the book, call it *flourishing* instead. Tech-wise parenting welcomes the mud, the crayon drawings on the wall, and the arguments, because it takes some messiness to flourish. After all, the creativity that makes a kid think the wall is her canvas also encourages her to sing cow songs—and to learn the violin.

Preface

The Proper Place

Of the many things I suspect my children will both thank me for and spend years in therapy recovering from, the phrase *proper place* is probably near the top of the list.

On the spectrum from cleanness-obsessed neat freak to junk-tolerant compulsive hoarder, I'm definitely at the neatness end. So as soon as our children were old enough to understand the phrase, I started drilling into them the idea that at the end of each day, or at least once a week—OK, well, at least when friends were coming over—the flotsam and jetsam of our family life should all be put back in its "proper place."

In a kind of demented version of musical chairs, we'd queue up ten minutes' worth of music and target one part of our home. At the end of ten minutes, everything that was out of place needed to be put back or, if its proper place was in another part of the house, put in a laundry basket commandeered for that purpose. Anything that was not in its place or in the laundry basket by the time the music stopped was to be summarily thrown in the trash. In the last moments before the music stopped, out-of-place books, homework papers, and beloved stuffed animals would all dangle menacingly over the trash can, to be rescued (most of the time) by laughing—or shrieking—children.

My "proper place" game, like so much in parenting young children, walked a fine line between effective and ruthless. More cleanup got done in ten minutes of music-fueled, trash-can-threatened frenzy than in days of halfhearted reminders. And at the end, Dad got a clean house, the stuffed animals were safely back in the bedrooms, and the children were only slightly traumatized. Of course, I never made good on my threats to put anything of real value in the trash—though the difference between what I and my children considered "of real value" will no doubt be further material for those future therapy sessions.

This book is about how to find the proper place for technology in our family lives—and how to keep it there. If only it were as simple as cleaning up a bunch of stuffed animals. Technology is literally everywhere in our homes—not only the devices in our pockets but the invisible electromagnetic waves that flood our homes. This change has come about overnight, in the blink of an eye in terms of human history and culture.

When previous generations confronted the perplexing challenges of parenting and family life, they could fall back on wisdom, or at least old wives' tales, that had been handed down for generations. But the pace of technological change has surpassed anyone's capacity to develop enough wisdom to handle it. We are stuffing our lives with technology's new promises, with no clear sense of whether technology will help us keep the promises we've already made.

That sense of overwhelmed uncertainty applies to the author of this book and to my own family. I can't possibly tell you how to handle the new app that your fifteen-year-old will want to install on her phone next week. I don't even know, honestly, how to handle all the technology my family and I already have (and I'm a certified geek who has loved technology ever since my dad brought home a "computer terminal" and modem in the 1970s—kids, ask your grandparents what those were).

But I do know this: if we don't learn to put technology, in all its forms, in its proper place, we will miss out on many of the best parts of life in a family. I've had the incredible, perplexing, and rewarding joy of parenting two children through the teenage years with my wife, Catherine—who is, by the way, a scientist who builds extraordinary technology in her lab and yet is incredibly sane in her lack of obsession with technology at home. As our children leave high school, we realize how much of the joy that we've experienced along the way, and know today, has come from the radical choices and commitments we made to keep technology in its proper place.

We haven't always made the right choices, and it hasn't always been easy. Some of what I'll share in this book comes from friends and mentors who had much more insight than we did, and much more courage. A lot of it is informed by our Christian faith, which gives us the clearest way we know of understanding who we really are and who, by grace, we are meant to be. What it all adds up to is a set of nudges, disciplines, and choices that can keep technology in its proper place—leaving room for the hard and beautiful work of becoming wise and courageous people together. Indeed, becoming wise and courageous is what family is really about—and it is what this book is really about, too.

This book wouldn't exist without my friends David, Roxanne, and their team at Barna Group, who urged me to write it and have been essential companions in the process. The researchers at Barna have been studying our culture, among youth and adults, for years. As we talked about what they were learning from both parents and teenagers, we realized that families have few more pressing needs than for guidance about how to handle the devices that have colonized our homes and our attention. One of the things I most admire about Barna Group is their commitment both to tell the truth about how we actually live and what we actually believe, and also to offer guidance for people who want something different from, and better than, the statistical average.

So the Barna team set out to document the role technology actually plays in American families and the concerns that both parents and children have about it. This new research is presented in these pages, with findings that are sometimes encouraging, sometimes unsettling, and always illuminating. Sometimes survey research can be used, subtly or overtly, as a form of peer pressure—see, everybody is doing it! But if there's one thing our children need to hear from us, over and over again, it's this: "Our family is different." Throughout this book you'll get a picture, from the graphs, charts, and sidebars, of the current reality of technology and family life, and a vision, from the text, of what could be a better way.

The proper place for technology won't be exactly the same for every family, and it is not the same at every season of our lives. One of my happy memories from my early twenties is of watching *Star Trek: The Next Generation* every Tuesday night with my roommate, Steve, cracking jokes at the plot twists and fighting over the chunks of cookie dough in the quart of Ben & Jerry's ice cream we consumed during the show each week. Twenty-five years later, given my other priorities, cotton-candy entertainment like *Star Trek* doesn't have a proper place in my weekly schedule—and a weekly half quart of premium ice cream definitely doesn't have a place in my waistline! In my twenties I could consume both, happily, and not have them interfere with my core callings and commitments.

So figuring out the proper place for technology in our particular family and stage of life requires discernment rather than a simple formula. Even the ten commitments in this book are meant to be starting points for discussion—and as you will read, they are ones my own family has kept fitfully at best. But almost anything is better than letting technology overwhelm us with its default settings, taking over our lives and stunting our growth in the ways that really matter. And I think there are some things that are true at every stage of life:

Technology is in its proper place when it helps us bond with the real people we have been given to love. It's out of its proper place when we end up bonding with people at a distance, like celebrities, whom we will never meet.

Technology is in its proper place when it starts great conversations. It's out of its proper place when it prevents us from talking with and listening to one another.

Technology is in its proper place when it helps us take care of the fragile bodies we inhabit. It's out of its proper place when it promises to help us escape the limits and vulnerabilities of those bodies altogether.

Technology is in its proper place when it helps us acquire skill and mastery of domains that are the glory of human culture (sports, music, the arts, cooking, writing, accounting; the list could go on and on). When we let technology replace the development of skill with passive consumption, something has gone wrong.

Technology is in its proper place when it helps us cultivate awe for the created world we are part of and responsible for stewarding (our family spent some joyful and awe-filled hours when our children were in middle school watching the beautifully produced BBC series *Planet Earth*). It's out of its proper place when it keeps us from engaging the wild and wonderful natural world with all our senses.

Technology is in its proper place only when we use it with intention and care. If there's one thing I've discovered about technology, it's that it doesn't stay in its proper place on its own; much like my children's toys and stuffed creatures and minor treasures, it finds its way underfoot all over the house and all over our lives. If we aren't intentional and careful, we'll end up with a quite extraordinary mess.

So consider this short book a bit like those ten-minute cleanup sessions I put my children through: a ruthless guide to sorting out where technology actually belongs in our homes and lives, and keeping it there. Like my kids, at certain points you may squeal in alarm as I seem about to throw away one of your most treasured possessions. But we'll get through it together, and at the end we might be a couple steps closer to the life we actually want—for ourselves, our children, and our children's children.

THE TECHNOLOGY-TROUBLED FAMILY

Parents believe raising kids today is more complicated than it was when they were kids.

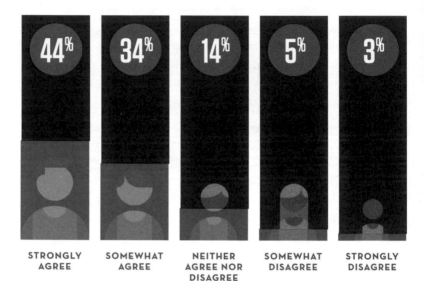

44%	34%	14%	5%	3%
STRONGLY AGREE	SOMEWHAT AGREE	NEITHER AGREE NOR DISAGREE	SOMEWHAT DISAGREE	STRONGLY DISAGREE

So, what is it that makes technology so challenging as a parent?

31%	30%	30%	30%	25%	20%
BALANCING PHYSICAL ACTIVITY WITH ONLINE ACTIVITY	LIMITING CHILDREN'S TIME WITH AND USE OF TECHNOLOGY	FILTERING CONTENT MY CHILDREN WATCH, READ, OR PLAY	WHAT MY CHILDREN ARE EXPOSED TO BY FRIENDS	FINDING FAMILY TIME WITHOUT TECHNOLOGY	MONITORING / WORRYING ABOUT MY CHILDREN ON SOCIAL MEDIA

n = 1,021 US parents of children ages 4 to 17

Why do they think parenting today is more difficult? Technology tops the list.

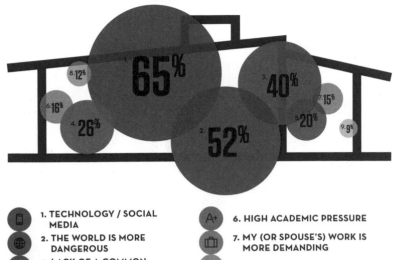

65% 1.

52% 2.

40% 3.

26% 4.

20% 5.

16% 6.

15% 7.

12% 8.

9% 9.

1. TECHNOLOGY / SOCIAL MEDIA
2. THE WORLD IS MORE DANGEROUS
3. LACK OF A COMMON MORALITY
4. FINANCIAL FACTORS
5. BULLYING AT SCHOOL
6. HIGH ACADEMIC PRESSURE
7. MY (OR SPOUSE'S) WORK IS MORE DEMANDING
8. LIVING FAR AWAY FROM FAMILY
9. AN EXPOSURE TO CULTURAL/ RELIGIOUS DIVERSITY

18% ACCESS TO PORNOGRAPHY

15% KEEPING UP TO DATE WITH WHAT TECH OR SOCIAL MEDIA MY CHILDREN ARE USING

15% MODELING HOW TO USE TECH WELL FOR MY CHILDREN

14% ONLINE BULLYING OR PRESSURE ON MY CHILDREN

8% MY CHILDREN "SEXTING" OR SENDING INAPPROPRIATE MESSAGES

2% OTHER

11% NONE OF THE ABOVE

Introduction

Help!

If there is one word that sums up how many of us feel about technology and family life, it's *Help!*

Parents know we need help.

We love the way devices make our lives easier amid the stress and busyness that fill our days. We love the way screens can, almost magically, absorb our children's attention and give us a few moments of quiet in the car or before dinner. We admire the ease with which our children master technology, the prowess they show with video games, the bursts of creativity in the arts, movies, and music that devices help them produce.

But we also sense the precious days of childhood are passing by, far too fast, in a haze of ghostly blue light. We watch as the inevitable intensity of teenage relationships is raised to near-toxic levels by a sleep-depriving, round-the-clock deluge

Technology Is the Number One Reason Parents Believe Raising Kids Today Is More Complicated Than in the Past

Raising kids today is more complicated than it was when I was a kid.

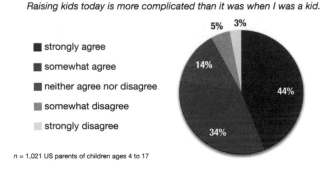

- ■ strongly agree
- ■ somewhat agree
- ■ neither agree nor disagree
- ■ somewhat disagree
- ■ strongly disagree

n = 1,021 US parents of children ages 4 to 17

of messages. We feel helpless to prevent them from over-exposure, far too early, to the most violent and intimate facts of life. (Medieval Jewish rabbis, it's said, used to discourage anyone under thirty from even reading the Bible's poetically erotic Song of Songs. If only *that* was our problem.)

Parents feel out of control, hopelessly overmatched by the deluge of devices. And we can't even count on one another to back us up. Parents who set limits on their children's use of technology often experience intense peer pressure—from other parents!

The kids know we need help too.

They see how addicted their own parents are to devices. Apple introduced the groundbreaking iPhone in 2007. An awful lot of children born in 2007, turning ten years old as this book is published, have been competing with their

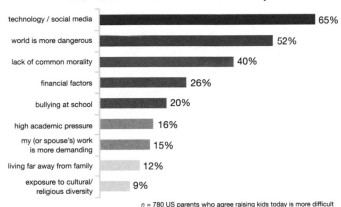

What makes it more difficult to raise kids today?

technology / social media	65%
world is more dangerous	52%
lack of common morality	40%
financial factors	26%
bullying at school	20%
high academic pressure	16%
my (or spouse's) work is more demanding	15%
living far away from family	12%
exposure to cultural/ religious diversity	9%

n = 780 US parents who agree raising kids today is more difficult

parents' screens for attention their whole lives. They see their parents tethered to their laptops, trying to stay ahead of work that has spilled out of the office into evenings and weekends. Older kids know the sick-to-the-stomach feeling of having binged on a video game for days on end (just as their parents know that queasy too-much-Netflix feeling). They've watched as their most media-savvy peers, the ones with a thousand followers from their high school or a million followers from all over the world, first expose themselves, then overexpose themselves, and go from reveling in the attention to breaking under the weight of others' expectations and derision.

To be a child, teenager, or young adult these days is to have to navigate a minefield of potentially life-altering choices, often with strangely little guidance from older adults, who are, after all, glued to their own screens.

They know there must be a better way.

And the grandparents? They aren't necessarily free of their own overdependence on technology, but I've heard more distress about our current technological addictions from grandparents than anyone else. They love their grandchildren—and, with slightly less infatuation, their children—and want to spend time with them, not just as young children but as middle schoolers, high schoolers, and beyond. But they see their grandchildren absorbed in their devices, preoccupied with popular entertainment and chatter with their peers, just when they could be having the time of their—and their grandparents'—lives. The grandparents most of all may know we need help.

Almost Almost Amish

There is a better way. It doesn't require us to become Amish, entirely separating ourselves from the modern technological world, and it doesn't require us to deny the real benefits that technology provides our families and our wider society. But let me be direct and honest: this better way is radical. It requires making choices that most of our neighbors aren't making. It requires making choices that most of our neighbors *in church* aren't making.

Let me put it this way: you don't have to become Amish, but you probably have to become closer to Amish than you think.

This better way involves radically recommitting ourselves to what family is about—what real life is about. Our homes aren't meant to be just refueling stations, places where we and our devices rest briefly, top up our charge, and then go back to frantic activity. They are meant to be places where the very best of life happens. No matter what advertising says (even those beautiful, tear-jerking Apple ads), the very best of life has almost nothing to do with the devices we buy. It has a lot to do with the choices we make, choices that our devices often make more difficult.

The good news is that it is absolutely, completely possible to make different choices about technology from the default settings of the world around us. I've seen other families do it—I'll tell some of their stories in this book—and my wife, Catherine, and I have done it, along with the (mostly!) enthusiastic participation of our children, Timothy and Amy (nineteen and sixteen years old as this book is published). I'll tell you about the bumps in the road along the way, for sure, but the main thing we all want you to know is that it is possible to love and use all kinds of technology but still make radical choices to prevent technology from taking over our lives.

Our family is radical, but we are definitely not Amish—although we love to eat the fruit, vegetables, meat, and cheese produced by our Amish neighbors forty miles away in Lancaster County, Pennsylvania. We find much to admire and learn from in the way they live with one another, their animals, and the land. As Nancy Sleeth puts it in the title of her wonderful book about a life lived in conscious resistance to technology's default settings, maybe you should call us "almost Amish."[1]

Or maybe "almost almost Amish." The number of Apple devices we collectively own is easily in double digits, and in the basement there's a pretty sweet TV, purchased just before those gorgeous plasma screens were phased out.

We eat home-cooked meals most nights, often by candlelight, which no one loves more than our kids (there is always an intense competition to be the one who lights the candles). On the other hand, the very night I type these words, my daughter and I shared a microwaved dinner—and a great conversation about her new semester at school.

We benefit from all kinds of devices, but we don't build our lives around them. We haven't eliminated devices from our lives by any means, but we go to great lengths to prevent them from taking over our lives.

Here's an example of that almost-almost-Amish approach: We chose not to have a TV at all in our house until our children reached double digits (more about that later). But we did buy that pretty sweet TV I mentioned when my daughter was ten. Eighteen months later, a friend who knew of our unusual lifestyle emailed me to ask how adding a TV was turning out.

"Amy," I asked, "how has having a TV changed our lives?"

She barely looked up from the book she was reading and said vaguely, "Do we have a TV?"

Build your life around not having a TV, and when you finally do have a TV, almost nothing will change.

Four Areas Emerge as Most Challenging for Parents

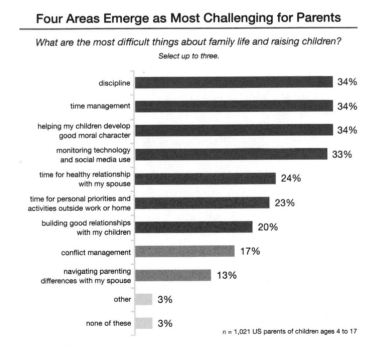

What are the most difficult things about family life and raising children?
Select up to three.

discipline	34%
time management	34%
helping my children develop good moral character	34%
monitoring technology and social media use	33%
time for healthy relationship with my spouse	24%
time for personal priorities and activities outside work or home	23%
building good relationships with my children	20%
conflict management	17%
navigating parenting differences with my spouse	13%
other	3%
none of these	3%

n = 1,021 US parents of children ages 4 to 17

Start to put the commitments in this book into practice, and if you have kids old enough to form the word "no," let alone to hack their way through the internet firewall, they will probably complain, loudly, for two weeks. *You* will complain, for two weeks. But very soon, you'll wonder why you ever waited this long to pursue the real life you were made for.

The Value of the Nudge

We didn't just hold off on buying a TV for our kids' sake. I find TV's moving images nearly irresistible. This is a problem in America, because in an awful lot of public places and homes, there's an awful lot of TV. If there is a screen in view, I'll find myself following a college basketball game, or, for that matter, local-car-dealer advertisements, with far keener attention than I'm giving to the person right across from me.

So I make it a practice to find a seat where I simply can't see a screen. I know I'm not capable of resisting the urge to watch, so I remove the temptation whenever I can, especially when there's a person with me who deserves my full attention. (That, of course, describes every single person who's ever been willing to share a meal with me.)

I suppose that I could try to change my own mental circuitry—perhaps through a program of desensitization, watching so many local-car-dealer ads that I lose interest in seeing another. Or I could try to build up my willpower or my ability to concentrate on a conversation in spite of distractions. Those would be worthy goals, and they might become necessary if screens become even more unavoidable. But to achieve that level of inner transformation would require time and effort. For now, I can almost always settle for simply sitting where no screens are in sight. It's a simple, low-friction decision that has made countless hours at friends' homes and at restaurants much more meaningful and memorable than they would have been otherwise. You might call it a *nudge*.

As popularized in Richard Thaler and Cass Sunstein's fascinating book by the same name, nudges are small changes in the environment around us that make it easier for us to make the choices we want to make or want others to make.[2] Nudges don't generally *make* us do anything, but they make certain choices easier and more likely. They don't focus so much on changing anything about our own preferences and ability to choose well; they simply put the best choice right in front of us and make the wrong choice harder. An increasing body of psychological research suggests that our supply of willpower—the ability to make hard decisions that go against our instincts or preferences—is limited. Nudges help us make some of those right decisions without having to use up that precious limited supply of willpower, leaving it available for the moments when we really need it.

The world around us is nudging us all the time. Restaurants arrange their buffet lines with the salad and soup (which cost the restaurant very little) ahead of the roast beef (which costs a lot). Grocery stores put the chips and soda (with their high profit margin) right in front of us as we shop, and they put the milk and eggs (which are often sold at a loss) at the back of the store. If an employer wants employees to contribute to a retirement plan, the participation rate goes up dramatically simply by asking them to opt out of the plan rather than opt in.

My wife, Catherine, who thinks a lot about how to get all of our family eating more healthy food, puts salad on the dinner table almost every night. I think it's fair to say that none of the rest of us, if salad were missing, would get up to go look for it (something we regularly do for ice cream). But with it sitting on the table, and with Mom passing it around, most nights we eat it. She doesn't insist, but she does nudge.

The makers of technological devices have become absolute masters at the nudge. Every notification that comes in on your smartphone is a nudge—not a command or demand, but something that makes it easier to stop whatever you're currently doing and divert your attention to your screen. Increasingly sophisticated algorithms help apps manage the number of nudges so you never get tired of responding to them. The mere presence of your smartphone in your pocket is a nudge, a gentle reminder that just a tap away are countless rewards of information, entertainment, and distraction. If you sit down on your couch and the TV remote is sitting in front of you, inviting you to press the power button and see what's on—that's a nudge. The TV itself is a nudge—if it weren't there at all, you'd have to go somewhere else (maybe out to dinner!) to watch a game or a sitcom or, for that matter, car-dealer ads. But with it sitting right there, it's easy to make the choice to stay put and turn it on.

We are continually being nudged by our devices toward a set of choices. The question is whether those choices are leading us to the life we actually want. I want a life of conversation and friendship, not distraction and entertainment; but every day, many times a day, I'm nudged in the wrong direction. One key part of the art of living faithfully with technology is setting up better nudges for ourselves.

Disciplines and Choices

Nudges, however, will never be enough. Nudges play to our weakness—our tendency to take the easy road most taken. They change the environment outside us in order to make good choices easier. But nudges will never, on their own, build the wisdom and courage we need—partly because we often can't control our environment, no matter how much we'd like to. We need to change something inside of us as well: to develop the strength to make good choices even when everything around us is nudging, or pushing, us in the wrong direction. And for that we need *disciplines*.

Disciplines are very much like what weight lifters call *progressive overload*. The best way to gain strength is by pushing your muscles to the very edge of their current capacity, for a relatively brief time. No one can spend twelve hours a day bench-pressing hundreds of pounds, and no one should want to. But spend an hour a day, a few days a week, in that kind of focused, strenuous exertion, and you will see gains in strength that come no other way, strength that will then be available for everything else you do. The point of working out is not just to be able to complete more reps with higher weight a few times a week—it's to develop and train our bodies to be healthier all the time. (Indeed, it seems that regular strength training, by building muscle tissue, helps us burn more calories even when we are sitting still!)[3]

This is how spiritual disciplines work as well. The central disciplines of the spiritual life, as taught by generations of Christian saints, have stayed the same for twenty centuries now: solitude, silence, and fasting. Each of them pushes us beyond our natural limits, and all of them give us spiritual resources for everyday life that we can't gain any other way.

Very few of us, for example, are meant to spend our lives largely alone, but the person who has not experienced or cannot bear *solitude* is missing an essential part of maturity. ("Let him who cannot be alone beware of community. . . . Let him who is not in community beware of being alone"—Dietrich Bonhoeffer.)[4] We are not meant for perpetual silence—we are meant to listen and speak. But the person who has not experienced or cannot bear *silence* does not understand what they hear and has little to offer when they speak. And of course we are meant to eat, and even to feast, but only when we *fast* do we make real progress toward being free of our dependence on food to soothe our depression and anesthetize our anxieties.

The disciplines, by taking us to our very limits, gradually move those limits. They move us toward being the kinds of people we were meant to be and want to be. So the discipline of Sabbath, for example, doesn't just help us take one day a week to enjoy deep and restorative rest (with all the preparation, concentration, and commitment that requires); it helps us make choices the rest of the week to avoid anxiety and pride.

The most powerful choices we will make in our lives are not about specific decisions but about patterns of life: the nudges and disciplines that will shape all our other choices. This is especially true with technology. Technology comes with a powerful set of nudges—the default settings of our "easy-everywhere" culture. Because technology is devoted primarily to making our lives easier, it discourages us from disciplines, especially ones that involve disentangling ourselves from technology itself.

If we want a better life, for ourselves and for our families, we will have to choose it—and the best way to choose it is to nudge and discipline ourselves toward the kind of life we most deeply want. We'll arrange the places we live and the patterns of our daily lives to make the best choice easier. And because the best choice often requires strength and courage, we'll build in periods of intense effort or demanding withdrawal that help us make the right choice when it's not easy at all.

So Here's the Plan

The rest of this book is about the commitments we can make toward that better life. I've suggested "ten commitments" for a healthy family life with technology—one in each of the following chapters. The ten commitments are definitely not the same as the Ten Commandments! Even though I recommend each one wholeheartedly, you'll discover as you read that our family has not kept all of them equally well. (Though the same is true, it occurs to me, with the Ten Commandments.) Your family may choose to emphasize a few of these commitments more than others, and perhaps to set one or two aside—and there may be other commitments that are important for your family that are not covered here. I offer these simply as a good starting point for nudging and disciplining ourselves in a better direction.

The ten commitments begin with three choices that are especially fundamental.

The first and deepest is to *choose character*—to make the mission of our family, for children and adults alike, the cultivation of wisdom and courage.

It's a complex, rapidly changing world, and parents today are feeling it. Nearly eight in ten parents (78%) believe that they have a more complicated job in raising their kids today than their parents did raising them. Monitoring technology usage tops the list of what they perceive contributes to this difficulty. Beyond that, parents seem to most often identify issues that feel out of their control and that are global in scope: a more dangerous world or a lack of a common morality. The consequences of these difficulties feel dire and so, perhaps, scare parents more than local or personal factors such as finances, bullying at school, or high academic pressures.

The second is to *shape space*—to make choices about the place where we live that put the development of character and creativity at the heart of our home.

And the third is to *structure time*—to build rhythms into our lives, on a daily, weekly, and annual basis, that make it possible for us to get to know one another, God, and our world in deeper and deeper ways.

So we'll begin, in the first part of the book, with those three basic choices, the foundation for everything else.

In the second part, we'll look at some nudges and disciplines we can put in place every day to have a healthier life with technology, from the moment we wake up until the end of the day.

And in the third part, we'll look at the two biggest tasks we were made for: to worship God with all our heart, soul, mind, and strength, and to care for one another at our most vulnerable—at our birth, at our times of great sickness, and at our death.

This book is about much more than just social media, or even screens. It's about how to live as full, flourishing human beings. Maybe it will even turn out that in that quest for flourishing, technology in its proper place can actually help.

Ten Tech-Wise Commitments

1 We develop wisdom and courage together as a family.

2 We want to create more than we consume. So we fill the center of our home with things that reward skill and active engagement.

3 We are designed for a rhythm of work and rest. So one hour a day, one day a week, and one week a year, we turn off our devices and worship, feast, play, and rest together.

4 We wake up before our devices do, and they "go to bed" before we do.

5   We aim for "no screens before double digits" at school and at home.

6   We use screens for a purpose, and we use them together, rather than using them aimlessly and alone.

 7   Car time is conversation time.

8   Spouses have one another's passwords, and parents have total access to children's devices.

9   We learn to sing together, rather than letting recorded and amplified music take over our lives and worship.

 10   We show up in person for the big events of life. We learn how to be human by being fully present at our moments of greatest vulnerability. We hope to die in one another's arms.

The Three Key Decisions of a Tech-Wise Family

THE VALUE OF FAMILY

7 in 10 parents say they have an explicit set of values for their family, but less than 3 in 10 have written out that purpose or mission statement.

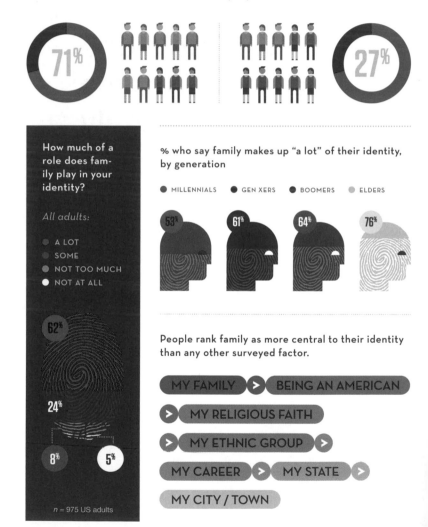

71%

27%

How much of a role does family play in your identity?

All adults:

- A LOT
- SOME
- NOT TOO MUCH
- NOT AT ALL

62%

24%

8%

5%

n = 975 US adults

% who say family makes up "a lot" of their identity, by generation

● MILLENNIALS ● GEN XERS ● BOOMERS ● ELDERS

53% **61%** **64%** **76%**

People rank family as more central to their identity than any other surveyed factor.

MY FAMILY ▸ BEING AN AMERICAN

▸ MY RELIGIOUS FAITH

▸ MY ETHNIC GROUP ▸

▸ MY CAREER ▸ MY STATE ▸

MY CITY / TOWN

PARENTS TAKE THEIR ROLE IN CHARACTER BUILDING VERY SERIOUSLY

How often would you say you talk about the following with your children?

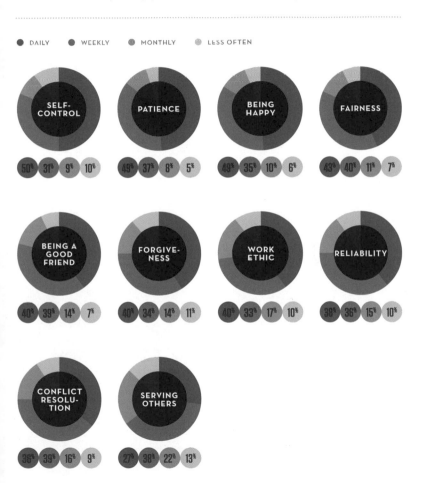

● DAILY ● WEEKLY ● MONTHLY ○ LESS OFTEN

SELF-CONTROL — 50% 31% 9% 10%

PATIENCE — 49% 37% 8% 5%

BEING HAPPY — 49% 35% 10% 6%

FAIRNESS — 43% 40% 11% 7%

BEING A GOOD FRIEND — 40% 39% 14% 7%

FORGIVENESS — 40% 34% 14% 11%

WORK ETHIC — 40% 33% 17% 10%

RELIABILITY — 38% 36% 15% 10%

CONFLICT RESOLUTION — 36% 39% 16% 9%

SERVING OTHERS — 27% 38% 22% 13%

n = 1,021 US parents of children ages 4 to 17; due to rounding, numbers may not add up to 100

1

....

Choosing Character

1. We develop wisdom and courage together as a family.

To understand how radical our approach to technology and family life needs to be, we need to understand what makes technology so different from any previous human invention or set of inventions—what makes it so radically new. We also need to understand what family is for, which is something radically ancient and in grave danger of being forgotten.

First, let's define what we mean by technology.

This is what makes our lives different from those of any human beings who have lived before us—including our grandparents and even our parents: technology works, and it is everywhere.

Now, there have been *tools* for as long as there have been human beings. But in this book I want to use the word *technology* for something more than just the tools human beings have always used. For almost all of human history, tools were quite limited. They weren't everywhere; they were in specific places. Tools were in the field (agricultural tools) or in the kitchen (cooking tools) or in the toolshed (work tools). And while tools *helped* us do our work, they didn't *work* on their own. The dream of a tool that would work by itself was strictly the stuff of magic or fantasy—the sorcerer's apprentice's dream of a broom that would clean up by itself.

Even though tools made human work easier, they weren't necessarily easy to use. Ask anyone who's tried to use a hammer skillfully, let alone a chain saw. Learning to use a tool requires patience and practice.

But we don't just live in the age of better tools—we live in the age of technology, which gives us completely new ways to get work done in the world. Quietly parked under a cabinet in our living room is exactly the kind of magical servant the sorcerer's apprentice dreamed about—a robotic vacuum that, once a week, emerges from its lair and sweeps up our first floor all by itself. (Its vacuuming is not perfect, and it does require a certain amount of maintenance, so it's not quite the magical dream the sorcerer's apprentice may have imagined, or indeed that we imagined when we bought it. On the upside, though, the sorcerer's apprentice's dream turned into a nightmare of multiplying, out-of-control brooms, whereas our robot, so far, has not spawned hundreds of maniacal robot minivacuums. Maybe that will happen with the next software upgrade.)

Increasingly, our lives have been colonized by things that don't just help us accomplish a task but do the task for us. And this technology, at its most beguiling, requires almost no effort or learning at all. (This will end up having a lot to do with what the role we think technology should or shouldn't play in education.) The highest compliment you can pay a piece of technology today is, "It just works!"

At the same time technology is less and less limited to a specific place. Take phones. Do you remember corded phones—where you had to go to one place in the house to use the phone? I grew up with phones like that, and even I can barely remember them.

Now, technology is everywhere. I don't mean just glowing screens and digital devices; I mean the whole apparatus of "easy everywhere" that has come into existence in just over the span of one human lifetime.

Modern technology has harnessed the invisible, high-energy electromagnetic spectrum, so it literally is washing over us and coursing through our bodies every moment. (Unless you wear a tinfoil hat—or suit.)

Modern technology is *in* our bodies—in the form of drugs and implants of various kinds, becoming more sophisticated every year, as well as the many hormones and polymers that leach out of human activity into the water systems, from there into the plants and animals we eat, and from there into our own bodies (and our children's). (Scientists looking at data from the National Health and Nutrition Examination Survey in 2004 found that 93 percent of subjects had traces of the plastic compound BPA in their urine.)[1]

For most couples in the modern world, technology is present during one of the most intimate and vulnerable experiences a body can have—77 percent of married couples in America routinely use contraception.[2] Our ancestors had ways of trying to prevent conception, but we have contraceptive *technology*, which both "works" far better (often without us having to think about it or even actively "use" it) and is far less intrusive or noticeable than our ancestors could have imagined.

Even what we consider "high technology" can progress from more tool-like to more perfectly technology-like. In its early days, the internet was more like a tool. People would "go online." It was someplace you had to "go." And it was finicky—slow and complicated. Now it just works. And it's not somewhere you go. It's like air. It's everywhere.

People often talk about science and technology in the same breath, but they are very different. I happen to be married to a scientist, and I know how hard she works to get her experiments to deliver accurate results, and how hard her students have to work to understand the mathematical underpinnings of modern science. In her lab, she and her students still work with tools—amazingly sophisticated ones, but tools all the same—that require training and effort to use well.

Technology emerges from the amazing success of modern science, and the hard work of scientists, but it's not like science at all.

Science is hard. Technology is easy.

Easy Everywhere

All this has happened, for all practical purposes, in about two generations. In the most fundamental ways, we are still like every other human generation that has ever lived. Like every generation before us, we are made for relationship with one another and with our Maker. Like every generation before us, we live in bodies that are both beautiful and burdensome. Thousands of years ago "Moses, the man of God" wrote these words: "The days of our life are seventy years, or perhaps eighty, if we are strong; even then their span is only toil and trouble; they are soon gone, and we fly away" (Ps. 90:10). Those words are as true for our time as they were for his.

But in one central respect, we are living a life that even our grandparents never imagined and could not fully understand: a world in which the technological dream of easy everywhere has come true—is coming true—before our eyes. In our grandparents' era, travel by air was rare, exclusive, and slightly dangerous; now it is one of the safest things you can do with your day. And it seems likely that in a few years another form of transportation will make a similarly grand leap from tool-like to technology-like, from requiring skill to working all by itself, in the form of driverless cars (which really will be, finally, *auto*mobiles, things that go by themselves). In our grandchildren's era, travel by car—currently one of the most dangerous things you can do with your day—may become as safe and passive as air travel is for many of us today.

We are in the midst of the greatest revolution in easy everywhere the world has ever known. And it may just be getting started.

All that would be fine—in its place, actually, it *is* fine.

It's just not the best thing for our families.

Here's why.

What Is a Family For?

I want to suggest a pretty radical idea about what family is for.

Family is about the forming of *persons*. Being a person is a gift, like life itself—we are born as human beings made in the image of God. But while in one sense a person is simply what we *are* as human beings, we are also able to *become*—to grow in capacities that are only potentially present within us at first.

Family shapes us in countless ways. But I want to focus in this book on two crucial qualities that family forms in us. Family helps form us into persons who have acquired *wisdom* and *courage*.

Wisdom is not just *knowledge*—mastering information about particular aspects of the world. Wisdom is understanding. It's the kind of understanding, specifically, that guides action. It's knowing, in a tremendously complex world, what the right thing to do is—what will be most honoring of our Creator and our fellow creatures.

This is why, in the psalms and the proverbs of the Hebrew Bible, the fool is the one who doesn't know God, doesn't understand fellow human beings, and doesn't even really know himself. ("A fool takes no pleasure in understanding, but only in expressing personal opinion" [Prov. 18:2]—which also sounds a lot like social media.) A fool can know a lot of things, but a fool doesn't really know what it is to be a *person*. And the fool certainly doesn't know how to act in a way that will serve the flourishing of persons—even, in the end, his own flourishing. The fool may be well educated, but the fool does not understand. When he acts, the results are, sooner or later, hilarious and disastrous in equal measure.

Two great things happen in families—at least, families at their best. For one, we discover what fools we are. No matter how big your house, it's not big enough to hide your foolishness from people who live with you day after day. We misunderstand each other, we misunderstand ourselves, and we certainly misunderstand God (when we remember him at all). In our families we see the consequences of all that misunderstanding. Our busyness, our laziness, our sullenness, our short tempers, our avoidance of conflict, our boiling-over conflicts—living in a family is one long education in just how foolish we can be, children and adults alike.

And yet a second amazing thing happens in families at their best. Our foolishness is seen and forgiven, and it is also seen and loved. As the British writer G. K. Chesterton put it in his book *Charles Dickens*, this is the secret of "ordinary and happy marriage":

> A man and a woman cannot live together without having against each other a kind of everlasting joke. Each has discovered that the other is a fool, but a great fool. This largeness, this grossness and gorgeousness of folly is the thing which we all find about those with whom we are in intimate contact; and it is the one enduring basis of affection, and even of respect.[3]

Somehow, in the discovery that we are great fools, we also begin to develop wisdom. This happened to all of us as we grew up, from children who foolishly thought every toy belonged to us, to adults who are capable of empathy and self-sacrifice. It happens for parents, too, as we discover in the course of caring for our children just how self-centered and impatient we can be and begin to acquire a deeper capacity for love.

All the really important things we do as families involve developing wisdom.

In some cultures, marriages are arranged by parents on their children's behalf. The decision about whom the child should marry is the culminating exercise of understanding the soon-to-be-adult son or daughter, their role in society, and the most fitting mate for their gifts and station in life. It's the final great exercise of wisdom by parents, summing up years of observing and investing in their children. Arranging a marriage involves a lot more than just knowledge, and it requires a seasoned perspective on life that young adults are thought not yet to have.

In North America, of course, most marriages are not arranged by parents, and marriage often happens long after children leave their parents' homes. But there is another process that many families go through in North America that has taken its place, one last arrangement of a child's life that requires a great deal of wisdom and is even more expensive than a wedding! It's making a decision about college.

My family, with our two teenage children, is in the midst of navigating the college search, application, admission, decision—and financing—process. To navigate through that complex process requires a great deal of *knowledge* on the part of everyone in the family. But the ultimate decisions about college require something more than just lots of information about colleges, applications, and financial aid. It requires that all of us, including the college-bound son or daughter, summon up all the wisdom (and money) we can.

Knowledge, these days, is very easy to come by—almost too easy, given the flood of search results for almost any word or phrase you can imagine. But you can't search for wisdom—at least, not online. And it's as rare and precious as ever—maybe, given how complex our lives have become, rarer and more precious than before.

The Faithful, Scary Thing to Do

If all we needed were wisdom, that would be challenge enough. But it's not all we need. Because we need not just to understand our place in the world and the faithful way to proceed—we also need the conviction and character to act. And that is what courage is about. The older word for this is *virtue*, a word that has dwindled, in our common language, into something like "niceness" or, worse, a kind of goody-goody avoidance of bad behavior. But we can't afford to give up the word's older and deeper meaning, which is the habits of character that allow us to act courageously in the face of difficulty.

Life is difficult. In fact, if you do life properly—with wisdom—life gets *more* difficult as you go. (Eventually, it gets difficult for everyone, especially for the ones who try to avoid difficulty.) And even though it's incredibly hard simply to know what we should do, it's even harder to actually act on what we know we should do. Because almost all the time, the most faithful, the most loving, and the wisest thing to do is scary, hard, and painful—even, in some ways, dangerous.

I knew—beyond the shadow of a doubt—that I was meant to marry my wife. That didn't stop me from lying awake long into the night before our wedding, praying through my anxieties and fears.

Later on, when we conceived our first child, we knew that our unborn child was a gift, but the months before his arrival brought excruciating sciatica for Catherine and the overwhelming challenge for me of loving my wife, who had been so healthy and fit and now was so limited and in so much pain.

At all the moments of greatest conflict in our marriage, and in our deepest friendships with others, the way of wisdom has been clear: stay committed, stay faithful, stay hopeful. To actually commit and keep faith and hope has sometimes asked more of us than we could imagine giving.

And we've been, on the whole, fortunate beyond belief in our lives so far. All of the hardest times are almost surely still ahead. We are old enough to understand that—we've seen friends walk through, and suffer through, all the heartache that life and death, loyalty and betrayal, can bring. We are wiser than we were when we were younger. But will we be able to bear whatever comes with the same grace and peace we've seen in others?

How can we become the kind of people who have wisdom and courage?

The only way to do it is *with other people*. We need people who know us and the complexities and difficulties of our lives really well—so well that we can't hide the complexity and difficulty from them. And we need people who love us—who are unreservedly and unconditionally committed to us, our flourishing, and our growth no matter what we do, and who are so committed to us that they won't let us stay the way we are.

If you don't have people in your life who know you and love you in that radical way, it is very, very unlikely you will develop either wisdom or courage. You may become smart, you might even become successful, but it is very unlikely you will have a deep enough understanding of yourself and your complex calling to actually become either wise or courageous. We just are too good at deceiving ourselves and think too highly of ourselves. The people who know us best see the truth about who we are, even as they also see more clearly who we could become.

Such people can be friends, to be sure. In adolescence, in particular, our friends play an important role in helping us develop wisdom and courage. But it is the very rare friendship that is extensive enough, intimate enough, and above all long lasting and committed enough to really uncover our deepest foolishness and cowardice and to draw out our deepest capacity for wisdom and courage. And the friendships that do make it to that level of honesty and commitment end up feeling an awful lot like family. Family, for almost all of

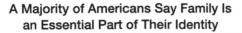

A Majority of Americans Say Family Is an Essential Part of Their Identity

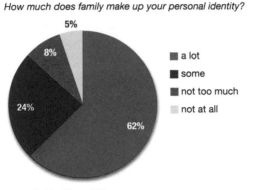

How much does family make up your personal identity?

- a lot
- some
- not too much
- not at all

5%
8%
24%
62%

n = 975 US adults; February 2015

us, is the setting where we are known and cared for in the fullest and longest-lasting sense. Family was there at your birth. If you are blessed, family will be there at your death. At the most vulnerable moments of your life, you hope that family will be there.

The First Family

This word *family* is potentially misleading, because what "family" means to us in places like North America is itself shaped by quite recent developments in culture, and indeed in technology.

It's only recently, and in a small corner of the world, that "family" has primarily meant a father, a mother, and their biological children living together in a "single-family" home. That may describe your own upbringing or your current living situation. (It happens to describe the situation of my wife, Catherine, and our children, Timothy and Amy, for the last decade or so.) But it may sound nothing like your life right now; indeed, according to the US Census Bureau it describes less than 20 percent of US households as of 2012.[4]

Either way, this book is for you.

Because while not everyone lives in a single-family home with kids underfoot, everyone has a family—or at least, in the plan of God, everyone can.

As a Christian, I actually don't believe the biological family is the main place we are meant to be known and loved in a way that leads to wisdom and courage. Jesus, after all, said some pretty harsh things about ordinary, biological family. He said that his way of wisdom and courage would divide children from parents and brothers from sisters—as it did in his day and sometimes still does in ours. When his own biological relatives came to one house where he was teaching and healing, trying to convince him to come home and stop being so messianic, he looked around and said, "Who is my mother, and who are my brothers? . . . Whoever does the will of my Father in heaven is my brother and sister and mother" (Matt. 12:48–50).

The first family for everyone who wants wisdom and courage in the way of Jesus is the church—the community of disciples who are looking to Jesus to reshape their understanding and their character. And the church is, and can be, family for everyone in a way that biological families cannot. No matter whether your parents are still living—or whether they were ever loving—no matter whether you have a spouse or children or siblings or cousins, you have a family in the church.

Of course, not all churches live up to this ideal—any more than all families do—but as our first family, the church is the place we learn to become the persons we were meant to be. This is surely why the very first Christians, who were not biologically related to each other and in fact came from entirely different ethnic and economic communities, referred to one another as *brother* and *sister*.

But if the church is to be our first family, it cannot just be a friendly, weekly gathering. The first Christians met in homes, and those homes were not single-family dwellings but Greco-Roman "households" that often included several generations as well as uncles and aunts, clients, and indentured servants of the "paterfamilias." The church too was a household—a gathering of related and unrelated persons all bound together by grace and the pursuit of holiness.

The house Catherine and I brought our son home to, nineteen years ago as I write, was not a "single-family" home. It was a three-story apartment that we shared with another married couple and two unmarried women, all of us brothers and sisters in Christ trying to be a little expression of the household of God in the city where we lived. Earlier, before we had children, Catherine and I had lived with other unmarried roommates; and before we married, we had each lived in intentional Christian communities with other women and men. (In one household I lived in after college, all five residents shared the same bank account for several years.) All of these homes were expressions of the "household of God," and all played crucial parts in forming us as persons.

So here's the complicated, wonderful truth. If our families are to be all that they are meant to be—schools of wisdom and courage—they will have to become more like the church, households where we are actively formed into something more than our culture would ask us to be. And if our churches are to be all they are meant to be, they will have to become more like a family—household-like contexts of daily life where we are all nurtured and developed into the persons we are meant to be and can become.

We've always needed a community wider than the solitary, nuclear family to thrive, and we surely need it now. Almost none of the commitments in this book can be realized by that minimal family unit. For technology, with all its gifts, poses one of the greatest threats ever conceived by human society to the formation of wise, courageous persons that real family and real community are all about.

Hollow Fruit

Please understand: I'm not saying technology is bad. In fact, I would say it is *very good*. Christians inherit the Jewish story in which the world is meant to be tended and developed by human beings, with their unique capacity for memory, reason, and skill. Once these image bearers were placed in creation, "God saw everything that he had made, and indeed, it was very good" (Gen. 1:31). Part of that "very-goodness" is the human capacity to discover and develop all the potential in God's amazing cosmos. It took thousands of years for us to understand how electricity and magnetism work together, to learn how to efficiently harness the earth's amazing reserves of energy, and to discover the properties of materials at tiny scales—but all that was there from the very beginning, waiting for us. Technology is the latest, and in many ways most astonishingly good, example of the fruit our image bearing was meant to produce.

But technology is only very good if it can help us become the persons we were meant to be. Let's honestly compare ourselves, and the society we currently inhabit, with previous generations who did not benefit from modern technology's easy everywhere. Without a doubt, compared to human beings just one century ago, we are more globally connected, better informed about many aspects of the world, in certain respects more productive, and—thanks to GPS and Google Maps—certainly less lost. But are we more patient, kind, forgiving, fearless, committed, creative than they were? And if we are, how much credit should technology receive?

I know this much: I cannot imagine working as hard as my grandfather and grandmother, who were dairy farmers

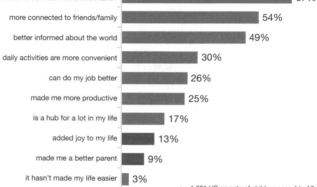

Technology Has Made Life Easier but Not More Joyful

In what ways has technology made your life genuinely easier?
Select all that apply.

access to so much more information	67%
more connected to friends/family	54%
better informed about the world	49%
daily activities are more convenient	30%
can do my job better	26%
made me more productive	25%
is a hub for a lot in my life	17%
added joy to my life	13%
made me a better parent	9%
it hasn't made my life easier	3%

n = 1,021 US parents of children ages 4 to 17

in western Illinois. They woke up before dawn every day and worked, for a sharecropper's less-than-minimum wage, nearly every day of their lives. Nor can I imagine being as thrifty as my grandmother on my mother's side, who went without luxuries and even necessities to save for the future, so that my college education (and my cousins') would be largely paid for.

In countless ways our lives are *easier* than our grandparents'. But in what really matters—for example, wisdom and courage—it seems very hard to argue that our lives are overall *better.* Perhaps, just perhaps, they are no worse. But this is exactly what we would expect if the things that really matter in becoming a person have nothing to do with how

Technology Has Made Life Harder

In what ways has technology actually made your life more difficult?
Select all that apply.

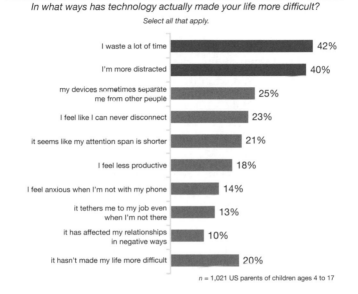

I waste a lot of time	42%
I'm more distracted	40%
my devices sometimes separate me from other people	25%
I feel like I can never disconnect	23%
it seems like my attention span is shorter	21%
I feel less productive	18%
I feel anxious when I'm not with my phone	14%
it tethers me to my job even when I'm not there	13%
it has affected my relationships in negative ways	10%
it hasn't made my life more difficult	20%

n = 1,021 US parents of children ages 4 to 17

easy our life is—and if they have a great deal to do with how we handle the difficulty that comes our way.

Technology's fruits are to be celebrated and delighted in. At this moment I am writing using a thoughtfully designed software program, displayed on a gloriously high-definition screen, powered by a refined and elegant operating system. On my ears are exquisitely balanced headphones that cost me just a couple hours' worth of wages, reproducing music that was created in part using advanced synthesizers and sequencers. It would be churlish to deny all the good that these technological gifts provide, let alone the easy-everywhere reliability of electric power and natural-gas-fueled heat on a December evening.

It's not just good—it's very good. But does it make me the kind of human being who could contribute something of lasting value to my family, my neighbors, my society, and our broken world?

Here is the heart of the paradox: Technology is a brilliant, praiseworthy expression of human creativity and cultivation of the world. But it is at best neutral in actually forming human beings who can create and cultivate as we were meant to.

Technology is good at serving human beings. It even—as in medical or communication technology—saves human lives. It does almost nothing to actually form human beings in the things that make them worth serving and saving.

Technology is a brilliant expression of human capacity. But anything that offers easy everywhere does nothing (well, almost nothing) to actually *form* human capacities.

Since forming our capacity to be human is what family is all about, technology is at its best a neutral factor in what is most important in our families. But it is very often not at its best, because we are very often not at our best, maybe especially in our daily lives with those closest to us. In the most intimate setting of the household, where the deepest human work of our lives is meant to take place, technology distracts and displaces us far too often, undermining the real work of becoming persons of wisdom and courage.

The Better Life

So here's where we have to start if we are going to live as flourishing families in an age of easy everywhere: we are going to have to decide, together, that nothing is more important

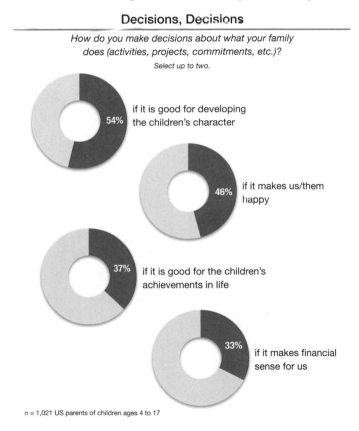

Decisions, Decisions

How do you make decisions about what your family does (activities, projects, commitments, etc.)?

Select up to two.

54% if it is good for developing the children's character

46% if it makes us/them happy

37% if it is good for the children's achievements in life

33% if it makes financial sense for us

n = 1,021 US parents of children ages 4 to 17

than becoming people of wisdom and courage. We are going to have to commit to make every major decision, and many small decisions, on the basis of these questions: Will this help me become less foolish and more wise? Will this help me become less fearful and more courageous?

We will have to teach our children, from early on, that we are not here as parents to make their lives easier but to make them better. We will tell them—and show them—that

Americans recognize the formational impact of family: the majority of Americans say their family is their main source of identity (62% say family makes up "a lot" of their personal identity, while 24% say it makes up "some"). With so much formative potential, how do parents approach goals and values in their family? The majority of parents (71%) agree that they have an explicit set of values guiding their family life, though few of them have written out a purpose statement or mission for their family (27%). Forming character in their children is a top priority for most parents: when faced with decisions as a family, the effect of the decision on their children's character is the top deciding factor (54%), with happiness being a close second (46%). Additionally, the vast majority of parents say they discuss issues of character (self-control, friendship, work ethic, conflict resolution) with their children on a daily or weekly basis. Technological advances have dramatically impacted parents, kids, and the family dynamic. Yet few parents say these technologies have helped them with the character formation they so value: only 13 percent say technology has added joy to their life, and even fewer say it has made them a better parent (9%). Parents are most likely to say, in fact, that technology has caused them to waste a lot of time (42%) and be more distracted (40%).

nothing matters more to our family than creating a home where all of us can be known, loved, and called to grow. And then we'll have to make hard choices—sometimes radical choices—to use technology in a very different way from people around us.

Making those choices will require wisdom and courage. But the rewards will be amazing.

Crouch Family
Reality Check

How well has our family done at putting wisdom and courage first, relationships at the center, and technology at the edges? Oh boy. I can't honestly say we've always done this very well. I, at least, have some awfully well-worn, comfortable patterns of growth avoidance. Some aren't technological at all—like my descent into exhausted inactivity on the nearest couch as a substitute for conversation with my family or with God.

Far too often, though, technology is at the center of my search for undemanding distraction. I find myself thumbing through Twitter or distractedly "liking" images on Instagram. Sure, there are other people at the end of those interactions, but they all too often substitute for my family. And then there are my one-hundred-plus nights of travel a year, made possible by technologies of modern transportation. Travel provides fulfilling work and helps me serve a wide audience, but such a lifestyle also diminishes my day-to-day chances for connection with my family, our neighbors, and our friends close to home.

When my family has made progress in matters of character, it has often come through the acute stress of conflict—the moments when our comfortable patterns break down and we find ourselves dealing with one another's overflowing emotions. I've been humbled into change by my children's pleading—or, in later years, their resigned disappointment—and by my wife's godly impatience with my passivity. (Is it just in our family that the male members seem more ready to use technology as a diversion, and the female members are more able to resist?)

I do believe Catherine and I are wiser than we were when we started our journey of marriage, and at moments I'm awed and thrilled to see our near-adult children making courageous choices informed by a gospel-saturated view of the world. But I sometimes wonder where we would be, and how much wiser and more courageous we would be, if we were not smothered so completely by technology's easy-everywhere embrace.

2

....

Shaping Space

> **2. We want to create more than we consume. So we fill the center of our home with things that reward skill and active engagement.**

The best way to choose character is to make it part of the furniture.

Fill the center of your life together—the literal center, the heart of your home, the place where you spend the most time together—with the things that reward creativity, relationship, and engagement. Push technology and cheap thrills to the edges; move deeper and more lasting things to the core.

This was once natural, indeed unavoidable. Almost every home once had a *hearth*, the fire that gave warmth, light, heat for cooking—and entertainment too, with its dancing flames and distinctive glow. The Latin word for hearth, *focus*, reminds us that fire was once the center of our homes.

Fire is a marvelous tool—one of the first human tools. But it is not *technology* in the sense I'm using the word in this book, with its easy-everywhere simplicity. Fire is dangerous and difficult to work with. Tending a fire, outside or indoors, requires skill, work, and care.

At the same time, fire is mesmerizing and beautiful. It is one of the only things in nature that glows on its own. Almost everything else merely reflects the light that comes from the fusion reactor conveniently located 93 million miles from our planet—still so bright that we can't look at it directly. But terrestrial fire generates its own light, and our eyes are drawn to it, watching it play and dance.

Today, we have furnaces instead of hearths. Furnaces warm our homes effortlessly, but they do nothing to concentrate our energy, relationship, attention, and delight the way the hearth did. They ask nothing of us (except prompt payment of the monthly heating bill) and they give us one simple thing: easy warmth everywhere. Reflecting their unrewarding and disengaged nature, we put them somewhere out of the way, in a closet or in a basement. Rightly so; a furnace is a boring thing, and usually ugly too.

But homes still need a center, and the best things to put in the center of our homes are engaging things—things that require attention, reward skill, and draw us together the way the hearth once did.

Gathering Spaces

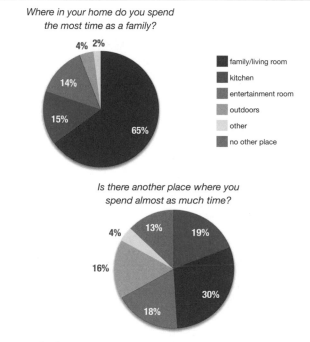

*Where in your home do you spend
the most time as a family?*

family/living room
kitchen
entertainment room
outdoors
other
no other place

4% 2%
14%
15%
65%

*Is there another place where you
spend almost as much time?*

13% 19%
4%
16%
30%
18%

n = 1,021 US parents of children ages 4 to 17

So here is a simple test of whether your home is a tech-wise space: find the place that is its emotional center—the place where your family spends the most time and the most energy—and take an inventory of what you see there. *Are the most visible things more like a hearth or more like a furnace?*

Spaces without Devices

Our own home is a smallish building, with three bedrooms on the second floor and an open living space on the first floor—living room, dining room, and kitchen all flowing together. We've worked over the years to arrange that space according to this chapter's commitment: filling it with things that reward skill and active engagement. When I stand in the middle of our first floor, here's what I see:

- works of art on the walls, most of them original work by friends whose craft and calling we want to support
- books—hundreds of books, even though we only keep the ones that are rewarding and worth rereading
- a few (impressively hardy) houseplants
- a grand piano and a string quartet's worth of instruments
- the space in front of the window where, through all of our children's early years, we had a wonderfully in-destructible "craft table" at a child's height, with art supplies, paper, and whatever project they were pursuing at the time (it's now in the attic, awaiting the arrival of grandchildren)
- a cabinet full of board games
- a fireplace we were lucky enough to acquire with the house

- a dining table, with candles on the table and in the chandelier overhead
- an oven and stovetop, which require someone to take the risk of creative cooking

What do these furnishings have in common? Some are basic and essential—the dining table and the stove. Others, like the art and the piano, are in one sense totally optional. But all of them require skill, sometimes a great deal of skill, to deliver their rewards.

Our house is hardly a technology-free zone, however. I can also see plenty of easy-everywhere technological devices:

- a charging station for our various electronic devices
- two pairs of bookshelf speakers, connected to a wireless music system
- a dishwasher
- a microwave oven
- invisible but vital radio frequency signals carrying cell and Wi-Fi data
- a refrigerator
- electric lighting
- heating and air-conditioning ducts, controlled by a thermostat

Where the Good Stuff Happens

Where do most leisure or entertainment activities happen in your house?
Select all that apply.

family/living room	79%
bedrooms	24%
outside	20%
kitchen	18%
home theater	10%
basement	7%
garage	7%
attic	3%
other	2%
our family doesn't	1%

None of these items requires us to have any real skill to use them, and each of them makes our lives more convenient without demanding much of us. There's plenty of easy everywhere in our lives and in our living room. The refrigerator, lighting, and climate control seem indispensable to us (though billions of people live without them today). The other items are awfully nice to have, and the music we play through our speakers often gives us genuine joy (and the occasional spontaneous sing-along).

Though our central living space is by no means technology-free (as if any space can be that in an age of Wi-Fi and cell

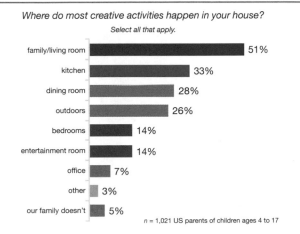

Where do most creative activities happen in your house?

Select all that apply.

family/living room	51%
kitchen	33%
dining room	28%
outdoors	26%
bedrooms	14%
entertainment room	14%
office	7%
other	3%
our family doesn't	5%

n = 1,021 US parents of children ages 4 to 17

phones), it is still true that *almost all the devices on our first floor can be—and regularly are—replaced by thoroughly nontechnological items.*

- The bookshelf speakers provide music, but we can also sit down at the piano or pull out the violin and make our own.

- We can microwave our meals (which is great for making the best use of leftovers), but we can—and mostly do—cook them from scratch. For that matter, while I love our built-in dishwasher fiercely, every night we also plunge our hands into warm water and wash the pots and pans by hand. (OK, actually it's usually the next morning. Or two mornings later.)

- Even the lights and the heat can be replaced by candles and fireplace. Some of our happiest times as a family have been spent on this first floor, lit entirely by candlelight and the glow of a wood fire. Why wait for a power outage?

- The Wi-Fi and cell signals are there, all right, but we can choose to ignore them, turning instead to conversation, music, books, or silence. Indeed, on Sundays (see the next chapter) that is what we intentionally do, all day long.

Only one significant technological part of life on our first floor can't be replaced by a nontechnological equivalent: *cold*—year-round refrigeration for our food and air-conditioning for sweltering summer days and nights. Everything else is turned off regularly.

And all the most beautiful and striking things—everything that would start a conversation or capture a child's attention—require our active engagement.

Priceless Things

The low-technology living room is not necessarily less expensive than the high-technology one (that grand piano wasn't cheap). But we could have the same kind of life for almost no cost—and when we were younger, we did.

Two pieces of art in our living room are by friends who happen to be renowned painters. The rest, made by friends and our own children, cost little or nothing and have no resale value—but emotionally, they are priceless.

Today we have a grand piano, but when we first married, our piano was an ancient upright, salvaged by a friend who wanted to practice her budding piano-technician skills. (In many parts of the United States, people will literally pay you to haul a piano away!)

Candlelit dinners cost no more when we were in our twenties than they do in our forties. The wood we burn in our fireplace was salvaged from trees that needed trimming or removing. Simple meals cooked from scratch cost no more than quick microwave dinners. Some nights the wine at our table was bottled in France, but many nights it comes from a box from Australia.

What makes the things on our first floor valuable is not their price. Instead, it's the way each thing asks us, our children, and our guests to bring creativity and imagination to life together.

So if you do only one thing in response to this book, I urge you to make it this: Find the room where your family spends the most time and ruthlessly eliminate the things that ask little of you and develop little in you. Move the TV to a less central location—and ideally a less comfortable one. And begin filling the space that is left over with opportunities for creativity and skill, beauty and risk.

This is the central nudge of the tech-wise life: to make the place where we spend the most time the place where easy everywhere is hardest to find. This simple nudge, all by itself, is a powerful antidote to consumer culture, the way of life that finds satisfaction mostly in enjoying what other people have made. It's an invitation instead to creating culture—finding joy in shaping something useful or beautiful out of the raw material of the world.

Children, in particular, are driven to create—if we just nudge them in that direction. They thrive in a world stocked with raw materials. But too often, and with the best of intentions, we fill their world with technology instead—devices that actually ask very little of them. A cheap electronic keyboard makes a few monotonous sounds, while an expensive one promises to make all kinds of sounds, from trumpets to marimbas to organs. But actually, neither the cheap keyboard nor the expensive one has anything like the depth and range of possibility of an acoustic piano—or a trumpet or a marimba (if you are considering filling your living room with an organ, you probably do not need to read this book). A single pencil can produce more "colors" of gray and black than the most high-tech screen can reproduce.

For a child's creative development, the inexpensive, deep, organic thing is far better than the expensive, broad, elec-

Most families do almost everything together in their family or living room. Two-thirds of parents (65%) say they spend the most time as a family in this space, with the kitchen coming in as the preferred second space. Entertainment, leisure, and creativity all overlap in this space—likely contributing to a presence of technology within all of these rooms. Families are most often participating in leisure or entertainment activities in the family room (79%), but it's also the place where families say their creative activities happen (51%).

tronic thing. And yet we are constantly tempted to give them toys that work on their own—that buzz and beep and light up without developing any skill. Why is this, when children of all people can invent more buzzes and beeps with their own lungs and tongue and teeth than any toy will ever make? Because we are infatuated by technology's magical character—and so are our children, briefly. But they quickly grow bored with devices that ask little of them and don't reward creative engagement, and their rooms and our attics become cluttered with the plastic castoffs that provided only one day's or month's worth of delight.

Skip the plastic, skip the batteries, skip the things that work on their own. Or, if they find their way into your home anyway, put them at the edges. In the center, put the things that both adults and children will find endlessly engaging, demanding, and delightful.

Crouch Family
Reality Check

Of all the commitments in this book, this is probably the one we have kept most consistently. My only regret is that increasingly, thanks to Wi-Fi, by the end of the day our first floor is often littered with laptops, tablets, and smartphones—and with family members staring at one (or more). But most nights, we clear everything away in time for dinner. Once again most everything in sight is organic, colorful, textured, with the fractal variety of nature—the wood of the chairs and table, the deep blue of the tablecloth, the motley patchwork of book covers on the shelves. The sleek blank slabs of aluminum and glass are banished for a little while. Like dust bunnies, they will accumulate if we let them, but at least we know they are not in their proper place. The heart of our home is built around things older and better than the newest thing.

3

....

Structuring Time

> 3. We are designed for a rhythm of work and rest. So one hour a day, one day a week, and one week a year, we turn off our devices and worship, feast, play, and rest together.

As technology has filled our lives with more and more easy everywhere, we do less and less of the two things human beings were made to do.

We are supposed to work, and we are supposed to rest.

Work is the fruitful transformation of the world through human effort and skill, in ways that serve our shared human needs and give glory to God.

Work requires wisdom—understanding something about the world, its limitations, and its possibilities. And work requires courage, because even work at its best involves risk and effort, and in a fallen world, work is not often at its best. Work also requires wisdom and courage because we always work *together* with others, and other human beings are never easy to understand or work with.

We are meant to work, but we are also meant to rest. "Six days you shall labor and do all your work. But the seventh day is a sabbath to the LORD your God; you shall not do any work—you, your son or your daughter, your male or female slave, your livestock, or the alien resident in your towns" (Exod. 20:9–10). One day out of seven—and, even more radically, one *year* out of seven (Exod. 23:10–11)—the people of God, anyone who depended on them or lived among them, and even their livestock were to cease from work and enjoy rest, restoration, and worship. They were called, you might say, to *ceasing and feasting*: setting aside daily labor and bringing out the best fruits of that work, stored up in the course of the week and the year, for everyone to enjoy.

This pattern is fundamental to human flourishing, and to the flourishing of the whole world that depends on our care, but it has been disrupted and distorted by human greed and sloth. Instead of work and rest, we have ended up with toil and leisure—and neither one is an improvement. And strangely enough, technology, which promised to make work easier and rest more enjoyable, often has exactly the opposite effect.

Toil and Trouble

Think of *toil* as excessive, endless, fruitless labor—the kind that leaves us exhausted, with nothing valuable to show for our effort. This is, alas, the kind of work that many people in our world must do their whole lives. But toil actually can afflict even the people who seem to have "dream jobs."

The journalist Dan Lyons, laid off from a position at *Newsweek*, found what he thought might be an exciting new calling at a technology start-up, an experience he describes with acerbic disappointment in his book *Disrupted: My Misadventure in the Start-Up Bubble.*[1] It was "one of those slick, fast-growing start-ups that are so much in the news these days, with the beanbag chairs and unlimited vacation," he wrote in the *New York Times*, "a corporate utopia where there is no need for work-life balance because work is life and life is work."[2]

But Lyons reports that the reality was more like "a digital sweatshop," with "glorified telemarketers" who "spent long days cold-calling prospects, racing to meet tough monthly quotas, with algorithms measuring their productivity."

The most poignant part of Lyons's essay, though, is the location where these (mostly) young adults toiled with no job security and pay just above the minimum wage: a former factory building for the Davenport furniture company. The name Davenport has become synonymous with some of the most beautiful pieces of human craftsmanship ever created.

In the "cavernous red-brick rooms" of that factory, Lyons recalls, "skilled craftsmen once labored on elaborately hand-carved custom pieces—woodworking treasures that today can be found in museums and in the White House."

Lyons recognizes that the artisans who made furniture in that factory undoubtedly worked hard. Their work was far more physically demanding, and because they lived and worked in the era before easy everywhere, nearly everything about their lives was difficult in a way that few of Lyons's coworkers have ever experienced. And yet their work created something of lasting beauty—"treasures." How likely is it that any of the employees who now work in that building are creating anything that will be seen as a treasure even five years from now, let alone five hundred years from now?

Instead of working, they are toiling—and of course, much-worse forms of toil can be found in our world. Millions of people employed in factories around the world today, let alone those who can find no work at all, would gladly change places with Lyons's fellow "digital sweatshop" employees. Still, what Lyons saw at that start-up is toil, not the fruitful work for which we were made. And this is happening at a successful, widely envied company that employs the most privileged winners of our society's rat race.

Toil is not new—it has been with humanity since the fall—and technology can be a tremendous resource for real, valuable work. From the recording studio to the operating room, technology at its best allows us to create and care for the world in marvelous ways. Indeed, one of the proper places for technology is at work, where advanced tools allow us to use our skills in ways that are personally rewarding and widely beneficial. But Lyons's story is a reminder that technology can just as easily double down on our toil, demanding more and more from us while we produce less and less of lasting value.

If technology has failed to deliver us from toil, it has done a great deal to replace rest with leisure—at least for those who can afford it.

If toil is fruitless labor, you could think of *leisure* as fruitless escape from labor. It's a kind of rest that doesn't really restore our souls, doesn't restore our relationships with others or God. And crucially, it is the kind of rest that doesn't give *others* the chance to rest. Leisure is purchased from other people who have to work to provide us our experiences of entertainment and rejuvenation.

A game of pickup football in the backyard can be real *rest* (as long as the competitive spirit doesn't get out of hand!). But watching football on TV is *leisure*, and not just because we're not burning many calories. It is leisure because we are watching others work, or indeed toil, for our enjoyment. It doesn't really matter whether the workers are well paid, like professional football players, or paid minimally and indirectly, like college athletes. From the point of view of the Sabbath commandment, it's still work.

Likewise, when we enjoy a nice restaurant meal on a Sunday, the enjoyment of that meal requires others to work. (Few people work, or toil, harder than restaurant workers.) If they have a regular day off on another day of the week, our leisure may not strictly require them to violate the principle of Sabbath. But even if their work is well balanced with rest, it's still leisure for us: rest that requires others to work on our behalf.

Of course, fruitless toil and fruitless leisure existed before the technological age. A tiny number of families enjoyed almost complete leisure, while many families worked without respite and collapsed, exhausted, for a few hours of sleep, day after day. Some societies, including our own, bought the leisure of a few at the price of the literal slavery of many. Slavery is the ultimate in fruitless toil, work that does nothing to benefit the workers themselves or allow them the dignity of passing on skill, rewards, and a better life to their children.

But in the technological age, toil and leisure are, oddly, less divided along these lines of social class. Many of us, even the most apparently privileged, have the uneasy sense that our work, though it seems physically undemanding (in its complete lack of physical activity, it may even be actively dangerous to our health), is toilsome. Most of us can now afford to purchase extravagant amounts of leisure—Netflix will sell you more entertainment than you could ever consume for $9 per month. But no amount of leisure can compensate for the sense that your life, whether poorly paid or well paid, is ultimately in vain.

Peak Leisure Home

The home used to be the location of both work and rest. In societies where almost everyone was a farmer or an artisan, most work happened in and around the home, often with the whole family involved—even today, child labor laws in the United States make exceptions for children who help with the family farm. Laura Ingalls Wilder's beloved Little House series depicts the backbreaking and difficult work—and indeed toil—of homesteading on the American frontier, but it also shows the family singing together to the music of the father's fiddle. The family would work hard, together, while it was day, inside and outside the house; then at dinnertime and in the evening, once the light had faded and work outside was impossible, they would rest together.

In the industrial age, the role of the home began to change. Work moved outside the home, into factories like the red-brick Davenport building. (In an era when industrial jobs were mainly reserved for men, this also meant that women's work became disconnected from men's and began to be treated as less valuable.) All that happened in the home was rest from the day of work—and, as affluence and technology increased, various forms of leisure. Maybe the high-water mark of leisure at home was that 1970s invention, the "TV dinner"—a prepackaged meal reheated and served in front of the television, the ultimate leisure device. Instead of conversation at a table set with a dinner prepared with care and often skill, the family "enjoying" a TV dinner had both their food and their conversation provided by others.

What happens to families when the home becomes a leisure zone? One of the most damaging results, as the philosopher Albert Borgmann has pointed out, is that children never see their parents acting with wisdom and courage in the world of work.[3] Even if the adults' jobs still require skill and insight, even if those jobs are quite meaningful and rewarding, that work now takes place far from home.

Technology also made much easier many of the forms of work that used to take place inside the house. I will admit that laundry probably never was much more than drudgery—though there is beauty and skill in a well-ironed shirt, something I still pride myself in being able to achieve. The technological magic that gives us washing machines, dryers, and noniron shirts can easily seem like a harmless improvement.

But when the art of cooking is replaced by meals warmed up in a microwave—something a five-year-old can do as well as a fifty-five-year-old—then children no longer see their mothers or fathers doing something challenging, fruitful, admirable, and ultimately enjoyable. Instead, the family's life together is reduced to mere consumption, purchasing the results of others' work or toil. No wonder children at the "peak leisure-home" stage of the 1960s and 1970s stopped admiring their parents. They never saw their parents doing anything worth admiring. (Is it totally an accident, by the way, that the 1970s gave us the "leisure suit"?)

Further into the technological age, the home has become the site of work—or toil—again. Many of us bring our work home on our screens. Parents and children alike can work late into the night, as kids download their homework assignments from the school website and as parents field messages from globalized, round-the-clock workplaces. But this is little like the era when children would watch, fascinated, as their mother or father demonstrated some skill, whether caring for farm animals, repairing a plow or an engine, preparing a pie or a roast, or turning a wrinkled piece of fabric perfectly clean and crisp.

Instead, the work that parents do at home, on our laptops and our phones, is hardly different from the schoolwork our children do—and sometimes much less obviously rewarding. As a young boy, my son told me he had figured out what my job was: "You type on your computer and talk on the phone." He didn't seem very impressed—and in one sense he was all too right. And I'm one of the fortunate ones who can bring fulfilling and rewarding work home. In a technological age, even those of us who have good work to do have to make an extra effort to show our children how our work requires real skill and produces something worthwhile.

Thou Shalt

Honestly, most of us can't do much to change the nature of our work—or toil. The demands of our industry, workplace, or profession are set by others and by complex social and economic systems. Few of us can entirely name our own terms of how, when, and where we will work. (Though if we can, there are few more important callings for us than to make our own work, and the work of those who labor for and with us, more fruitful, sustainable, and rewarding.)

But there is one thing most of us can do—and all of us are meant to do. It is to rediscover rest: real rest, in harmony with one another, our Creator, and all of creation. The biblical word for this kind of rest is *Sabbath*.

Sabbath appears in the very beginning of the Bible: on the seventh day of creation God himself "rested" from all the work he had done. Many of the Ten Commandments, the "thou shalt nots," address the distortions of fallen humanity—our tendency to make idols, betray and lie, murder and covet, all rooted in our persistent human desire to have other gods before the true God. But keeping Sabbath, along with honoring our father and mother, is one of the "thou shalts"—one of the positive things we would have been called to do even if we had never fallen into sin. Like family itself, Sabbath is rooted in the loving and creative purposes that brought the world into being.

Alas, of all the commandments, the Sabbath command may be the most persistently and casually broken. Just one generation ago, very few people went to work on a typical Sunday in America (except, of course, pastors!). Even now, fewer of us have to go to work on Sunday than other days. Some professional workplaces, notorious for their round-the-clock schedules, have even mandated a day off for their junior staff—Goldman Sachs and other New York financial firms introduced "protected weekend" policies in the early 2010s that are supposed to keep at least part of the weekend free from work demands.[4] But for more and more of us, Sunday can easily become another workday. If you work at Starbucks, you're as likely to be given a Sunday shift as any other day. And even if your workplace is technically closed on Sunday, thanks to technology, work follows us everywhere we go, every hour of every day.

And just as work (or toil) follows us into our day of rest, so does leisure. Netflix is always waiting to stream more entertainment into our home. Facebook keeps serving up more morsels of news, animated GIFs, and cute cat videos from our friends. It's easy to let Sunday become one more day of toil and leisure (maybe, if we're a churchgoing family, with the added stress of getting the whole family out the door at the same time in the morning, slightly better dressed and more polite than usual).

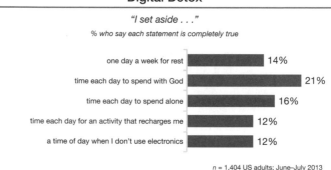

Digital Detox

"I set aside . . ."

% who say each statement is completely true

one day a week for rest	14%
time each day to spend with God	21%
time each day to spend alone	16%
time each day for an activity that recharges me	12%
a time of day when I don't use electronics	12%

n = 1,404 US adults; June–July 2013

Into the Wide World

But there is a silver lining in the way technology has clouded our lives with nonstop toil and leisure—it gives us an amazingly simple way to bring everything to a beautiful halt. We can turn our devices off.

Close the laptop. Slide the little onscreen button on your phone to the right and watch its screen go not just blank but black.

For bonus points, unplug the power strip that keeps all your entertainment devices constantly listening, like hovering ghosts, for the silent voice of the remote control.

Suddenly, with the flick of a few switches, you have left the world of technology—at least its most commanding and demanding forms—entirely behind.

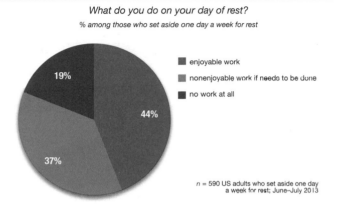

What do you do on your day of rest?
% among those who set aside one day a week for rest

■ enjoyable work
■ nonenjoyable work if needs to be done
■ no work at all

19%

44%

37%

n = 590 US adults who set aside one day
a week for rest; June–July 2013

Your home is now eerily quiet—not so much aurally as visually. Nothing is glowing—you are back in the visual world human beings lived in for millennia, where almost all light was reflected rather than transmitted. Nothing is blinking or buzzing at you, and for the next few hours, nothing will.

Now, consider your options. The wide world is outside your door. Maybe it's time for a walk, a run, a visit to the park or the playground. (At the playground, with phones left behind, parents may have to actually play too, rather than just hover at the edge tending to their devices while their children enjoy the fleeting years of physical engagement with dirt and grass and sky.)

Electronic Sabbaths?

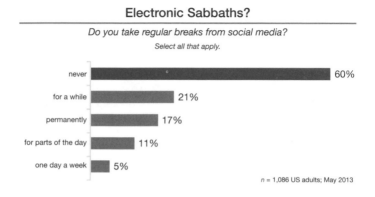

Do you take regular breaks from social media?

Select all that apply.

never	60%
for a while	21%
permanently	17%
for parts of the day	11%
one day a week	5%

n = 1,086 US adults; May 2013

Or maybe the weather outside is not appealing. There are still options—good ones.

There are books, some of them full of stories (leave the heavy-duty nonfiction for the rest of the week). Maybe it's time to sit with one for longer than you normally would, or to read one aloud together.

Or there is the kitchen—maybe today is the day not just for one parent to rush nutrition to the table but to make something together, fresh bread or cookies or a roast or soup, that takes time and is actually rewarding to prepare. (Don't forget the responsibility of cooks and children alike to sneak some tastes of cookie dough along the way!) Since (based on commitment number two) you have structured the central, most welcoming space of your home around the kinds of creative engagement that your family loves best, and with the screens dark around the edges of the house, the family will slowly but surely gravitate to that center. Especially if there are cookies.

Now, whatever the nature of your work during the week, you'll be doing something both demanding and rewarding, restful and rejuvenating—something adults can enjoy and children can admire and aspire to learn.

And then, just as the Sabbath commandment expands to include not just parents and children but servants and immigrant neighbors, find ways to invite others along for the joy of refreshment and rest. One of our treasured family traditions is Sunday afternoon tea, a custom loosely borrowed from our British ancestors that is easier to prepare than a full Sunday dinner. Our daughter makes place cards and hand letters a menu. We slice up fruit, bake cookies and bread, make little sandwiches, brew a pot of tea (and maybe pour some still or sparkling wine along the way, too)—and many Sundays we invite friends or neighbors to join us. The adults love the lack of pressure to deliver (or clean up after) a hot meal, the children love a meal composed entirely of snacks, and we all love the conviviality of passing simple, tasty treats around the table, and around again.

This is meant to be—commanded to be—our life, one day a week and more. A life of abundance, gratitude, rest, and quiet. It will only happen if we choose it, but if we choose it, the experience of our family and many friends has been that God blesses it.

One Day a Week—and More

We think of Sabbath as a day, but in fact Sabbath was not just a day but an organizing principle for the Jewish people. It was a pattern of life that extended to the "Sabbath year," one year every seven where fields lay fallow and the people were commanded to rest and worship, and to the "Jubilee year," one year every forty-nine where debts were forgiven and indentured servants were freed. (I wrote more about this "Sabbath ladder" in my book *Playing God: Redeeming the Gift of Power.*)[5] For us, too, Sabbath will be most powerful and helpful if we let its core pattern of work and rest become the defining pattern of our lives.

So I suggest a simple, minimal pattern of Sabbath: we choose to turn our devices off *not just one day every week but also one hour (or more) every day and one week (or more) every year.*

Build into every single day an hour, for everyone in the household, free from the promises and demands of our devices. For many of us, this will most naturally be the dinner hour. Few Americans, of course, sit at a weeknight dinner for a whole hour, but if we weren't springing up from food hastily scarfed down to get back to the demands of homework and leftover office work, maybe our dinners would last a few minutes longer. However long we're actually at the table, make it a daily practice to gather up the devices at the beginning of the hour, plug them all in (where they can

Dinnertime

How many times per week does your family intentionally eat a meal together, either in your home or at a restaurant?

6.3 times per week on average

Do family members bring phones or other devices to meals?

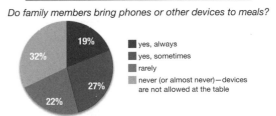

- yes, always
- yes, sometimes
- rarely
- never (or almost never)—devices are not allowed at the table

n = 1,009 US parents of children ages 4 to 17 who have family meals together at least once a week

How often do you or your spouse take calls or texts or do something else on your phone at the table during a family meal?

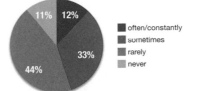

- often/constantly
- sometimes
- rarely
- never

n = 683 US parents of children ages 4 to 17 who bring phones or other devices to meals

How often do your children take calls or texts or do something else on their phone at the table during a family meal?

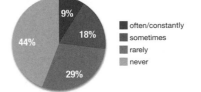

- often/constantly
- sometimes
- rarely
- never

n = 683 US parents of children ages 4 to 17 who bring phones or other devices to meals

have their own little feast on electrons), and leave them there, silenced and untouched, for sixty minutes. For families with small children, the better hour may be the hour just before bedtime, where baths and stories and cuddling can happen without digital distraction.

At the other end of the time scale, there are very few better gifts we could give ourselves and our families than an entire week—at the very minimum—free of devices. Our family has had the great privilege of being able to take two solid weeks of vacation each summer while our children were growing up. On the Friday before that vacation, I clean out my email inbox, set up a filter that will send every single message straight to an archive, and activate a "vacation message" with the stark subject line, "Unfortunately I will never read your email."

And it is gloriously true. For two solid weeks, my inbox stays completely empty. (Part of true rest is not having work accumulate relentlessly while you are resting!)

The days that follow are full—full of rest rather than work. We fill them with biking and hiking and grilling and reading and napping. Thanks to this annual Sabbath, we have memories of life together at every stage of our children's lives, memories that we will remember longer than anything anyone might email me about during those two weeks. When I return after two weeks and deactivate the filter, my empty inbox quickly begins to fill again. But I have had two weeks of rest. Somehow the work ahead, and the year ahead, seems more like gift and less like toil than it did before my digital Sabbath.

The Brightly Lit Cage

Not everyone can take two weeks entirely off from work, as my wife and I can. Even fewer *believe* they can. But we need to be clear: Sabbathless toil is a violation of God's intention for our lives and our whole economy. When we find ourselves in its grip, it means that we are slaves to a system of injustice. Sometimes that slavery is external to us and all too real—we are genuinely bound to systems of toil that prevent us from a healthy life, with no good option for escape.

This is certainly true for countless people in our world— not just those who toil at the very edge of subsistence in poor countries but also those who have to take multiple jobs to make ends meet in rich countries. Any serious commitment to Sabbath involves doing our best to ensure that the people who serve us—especially those who serve out of sight, not just the waitress but the dishwasher, not just the store cashier but the nightshift cleaning crew—are provided wages and benefits that allow for hourly, weekly, and yearly rhythms of rest.

But there is another form of slavery to systems of injustice, and that is the slavery of the imagination. Many of us are not as captive to round-the-clock, never-ending demands as we believe we are. Instead, we are our own jailers. We are prisoners of our own insecurity (Will I still have a job if I take two solid weeks of vacation?), pride (How can people get along without me?), fantasies (What if I miss an email telling me I've won the lottery?), and cultural capitulation (This is just how the world works now, isn't it?). For us, the door to a better life is only locked from the inside. We prefer our brightly lit cage of toil and leisure (this cage, after all, comes with unlimited Netflix).

In this area, as in all of life, the path toward real freedom—including the freedom to actually choose freedom, rather than imprisoning ourselves in our too-small substitutes for real life—is to embrace disciplines. And that is what the practice of Sabbath, whether on a daily, weekly, or yearly basis, can be. The beautiful, indeed amazing, thing about all disciplines is that they serve as both diagnosis and cure for what is missing in our lives. They both help us recognize the exact nature of our disease and, at the very same time, begin to heal us from our disease.

The disease of toil and leisure goes all the way back to our first human parents. Technology makes it more acute and damaging. Fortunately, our devices still have an off switch (at least most of them, and at least for now). Once we have made the choice to give our devices a rest—once we have gotten over the crucial, core discomfort of declaring that we will not attend to them for extended periods, every single day, week, and year—we are far more likely to live with them in restful ways the rest of the time.

Legalism and Work

By the time of Jesus, the pursuit of religious Sabbath obser-
vance had become its own kind of toil, a demanding set of
rules and obligations. "The sabbath was made for humankind, and not humankind for the sabbath," Jesus told the
Pharisees (Mark 2:27). The biblical prohibition on work was
life giving, but the thicket of rules about what exactly counted
as "work" ended up being so dense and forbidding that the
Pharisees were scandalized when Jesus healed the sick on the
Sabbath. Something has gone wrong with our disciplines
when we become more obsessed with the mechanics and
mechanisms of fulfilling them than with the gift they are
meant to give.

So we should be wary of legalism in the way we implement
our hour, day, or week of (relative) technological freedom.
But for most of us, the risk of legalism is far, far less of an
issue than our nearly insatiable appetite for the easy everywhere that technology offers. When it comes to technology, most of us are more like alcoholics than we are like
sourpussed teetotalers—and most of us desperately need
an infusion of intentionality about technology into our lives
more than we need release from overly limited, legalistic
restrictions.

When the Pharisees complained about Jesus doing
"work" by healing on the Sabbath, he pointed out that any
of them would (rightly) do the "work" of rescuing an ox,

True rest seems elusive for most Americans. Only one in seven adults (14%) set aside a day a week for rest. And on that one day a week, what do they do? Mostly, they work. More than four in ten say they do enjoyable work, and an additional nearly four in ten (37%) say they'll do nonenjoyable work if it needs to be done. Only one in five (19%) say they don't do any work at all on their day of rest. Even fewer Americans commit to daily time alone (16%) or with God (21%) or to activities that recharge them (12%). And when it comes to putting down those devices, only 12 percent of adults say they intentionally set aside a time of day when they don't use electronics. A full six in ten adults say they've never taken a break from social media, and only one in five say they have done so "for a while." When it comes to mealtime, though (parents, on average, say their family eats together at least six times a week), parents are more likely to insist on putting away devices. About one-third of parents (32%) say devices are not allowed at the table, and another one in five (22%) say family members rarely bring their devices to the table. Only one in five (19%) say their family members always bring their devices to the table.

let alone a child, that fell into a well on the Sabbath day. By all means, if technology will help us rescue someone who falls into a well, we should use it—even if it is during our precious week of vacation once a year. But we are already constantly telling ourselves how much we want to use technology for good. We are probably more at risk of being so distracted by our devices that we would fall into a well ourselves.

So one hour a day, one day a week, one week a year—set it all aside.

.... Crouch Family ....
Reality Check

When I think about our family's practice of daily, weekly, and yearly Sabbath, the phrase that comes to mind is, "It could be a lot worse." Our annual vacation really is completely, totally, and joyfully email and social-media free— though our screens do come along (for tasks like checking weather, tracking bike rides, and planning recipes), and there are times when they turn from servants of our creativity into the same kinds of tedious distractions they are at home.

Sundays, too, are more often than not truly free of work and glowing rectangles. But I find myself too often letting Sunday slide from *rest* into *leisure*. Often that means mindlessly picking up a tablet to aimlessly read the news or peruse sports stories—even though I can, and do, indulge in that kind of leisure activity any day of the week—leaving the unique, screen-free possibilities of Sunday unexplored.

And as for the one hour a day, we do keep our dinner table free from devices. At least until the plates are mostly clear. Then, many nights, a trivia question or a family scheduling decision prompts someone to bring a device to the table. Sometimes the question is quickly answered and the device is shut off; other times it leads one or more of us into distraction. It's rarely a full hour before the accumulated stress of the day propels us into the evening's schoolwork, office work, and housework. But for at least a short time, we had a taste of the life we were meant for: conversation, conviviality, communion. It's just enough.

Daily Life ②

TECH AROUND THE CLOCK

On average, parents say their children spend 5 hours using an electronic device on a typical weekday.

GOOD MORNING

62% ... of parents check their phone within the first hour of the morning. *And what are they doing on the phone in that first hour of the day?*
Select all that apply.

74% CHECKING EMAIL

51% SENDING OR READING TEXTS

48% CHECKING SOCIAL MEDIA

36% READING THE NEWS

24% CHECKING/ORGANIZING CALENDAR

17% USING A BIBLE OR DEVOTIONAL APP

10% WATCHING VIDEO

6% LISTENING TO AUDIOBOOK OR PODCAST

6% NONE OF THESE

GOOD AFTERNOON

After school, kids spend most of their time . . .
Select all that apply.

65% DOING HOMEWORK

64% WATCHING TV OR MOVIE

56% ENGAGING WITH FAMILY MEMBERS

42% PLAYING VIDEO GAMES

39% INFORMAL PLAY OR ACTIVITY

32% READING OTHER THAN FOR HOMEWORK

27% ON SOCIAL MEDIA OR TEXTING WITH FRIENDS

25% DOING EXTRACURRICULAR ACTIVITIES OR CLASSES

25% ONLINE OTHER THAN FOR HOMEWORK

23% PLAYING ORGANIZED SPORTS

22% HANGING OUT WITH FRIENDS

8% READING THE BIBLE / DEVOTIONS / PRAYER

GOOD EVENING

More than 4 in 10 parents say electronic devices are a significant disruption to family meals.

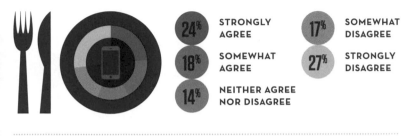

24% STRONGLY AGREE

18% SOMEWHAT AGREE

14% NEITHER AGREE NOR DISAGREE

17% SOMEWHAT DISAGREE

27% STRONGLY DISAGREE

GOOD NIGHT   *What's the last thing parents do before bed?*

31% WATCH TV

10% CHECK SOCIAL MEDIA

3% SPEND TIME READING ONLINE

2% PLAY A VIDEO GAME

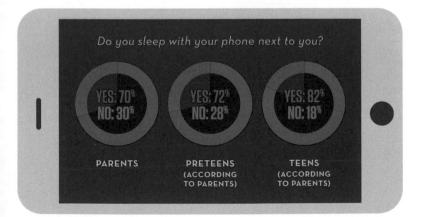

Do you sleep with your phone next to you?

YES: 70% NO: 30%
PARENTS

YES: 72% NO: 28%
PRETEENS (ACCORDING TO PARENTS)

YES: 82% NO: 18%
TEENS (ACCORDING TO PARENTS)

n = 1,021 US parents of children ages 4 to 17

4

....

Waking and Sleeping

4. We wake up before our devices do, and they "go to bed" before we do.

If there is one thing that sums up the difference between human beings and our technological devices—and, just as importantly, between us and our Creator—it is this: we need sleep. Lots of sleep. We are meant to be still, quiet, unconscious, and vulnerable for roughly a third of every day, and more when we are young.

Devices do not need this kind of rest. While anything with moving parts requires periodic maintenance, and even fully electronic devices will eventually wear out and fail, most of our technology can function for days, months, or even years without anything like sleep.

But we are not devices; we are persons. And while we are made in the image of God, in this respect we are not like God at all. God "never slumbers or sleeps" (Ps. 121:4 NLT) but is continually present and available to all creation. God's unsleeping care is good news: we sleepy creatures can trust that our needs will be provided for while we can do nothing on our own behalf.

Why exactly sleep is so fundamental is still largely a mystery. But we know that at least part of the puzzle is our brains' need to maintain the complex and delicate neural connections that allow us to build memory and skill. While we are apparently dead to the world, our brains are in fact buzzing with activity, recording memories, consolidating what we've learned and experienced, and cleaning up the biochemical residue of each day. It is not just visual or verbal memories that are encoded during these nightly sessions but physical ones as well. Athletic and musical skill, which require sophisticated neuromuscular coordination, advance dramatically with a good night's sleep. Sleep seems, in a strange way, to be where the learning required to be accomplished human beings actually happens. It is the way our bodies deal with the immense complexity and demands of growth of all kinds— intellectual, physical, emotional, and even spiritual. Heart, mind, soul, and strength all are nurtured while we sleep.[1]

And thus sleep is absolutely essential to human flourishing. Depriving someone entirely of sleep is one of the cruelest forms of torture and leads rapidly to physical, mental, and emotional breakdown. Even simply fighting off our own bodies' urge to fully rest for a few nights incurs what psychologists call "sleep debt." Sleep debt cannot be written off or powered through—it eventually must be repaid, and while it remains outstanding, it has dramatic effects on our cognitive and physical capacities.

Perhaps all this is in the background of the ancient Jewish and Near Eastern practice of considering sunset the start of the day, instead of sunrise. The Jewish people's psalms included this heartening admonition: "It is in vain that you rise up early and go late to rest, eating the bread of anxious toil; for he gives sleep to his beloved" (Ps. 127:2). A Jewish day begins in the quietness of dusk, sharing the evening meal as the world settles in to rest, lying down to practice the "quietness and confidence" that Isaiah said was the source of true strength (Isa. 30:15 NLT). And then in the morning (neither anxiously early nor slothfully late) we rise to our work. Rather than resting to recover from a hard day's work, this way of seeing time suggests that we work out of the abundance of a good night's rest.

Bright Nights

Providing an environment for sleep—a place where we can rest, ideally undisturbed and unafraid—is one of the most basic functions of home. Work, meals, entertainment, social life—all these can happen outside our home. But almost all of us settle into our own beds at night (and those of us who travel rarely sleep as well anywhere else).

One of the early and most demanding tasks of parenting is helping children sleep, beginning with the rocking, walking, singing, and even vacuuming (the only thing that worked for my own parents when I was an infant!) that help calm babies who haven't yet learned to calm themselves. For many years to come, parents settle down next to their children's beds, reading stories or saying prayers or singing lullabies. And then we turn to our own beds. Some nights we collapse quickly in exhaustion (especially in the early, sleep-deprived days of parenthood); other nights we try to quiet our own rehearsing of the day that is past and anxieties about the day to come.

But nothing about our lives at home has been so thoroughly disrupted by technology as sleep. The disruption began with the first wave of technology, widespread electrification that allowed lights to burn steadily and brightly in our homes well after it was dark. The expression "burning the midnight oil" comes from a pretechnological time when keeping a lamp lit was a costly and unusual practice. Even with a lamp lit, earlier generations would be prepared consciously and unconsciously for bed and rest, with the circle of light reduced to a small space in the wider darkness. But now, a flip of a switch allows us to flood our homes with light.

Like almost all technology, illumination on demand—with technology's signature qualities, easy and everywhere—is in many ways a gift. But it is also a powerful nudge in the wrong direction, and as a result many of us are chronically deprived of sleep and its benefits. And the problem is compounded by the portable communication devices—laptops, tablets, and above all cell phones—which are now within reach day and night.

It may also turn out to be true, as some studies seem to show, that the bright blue light given off by most device screens

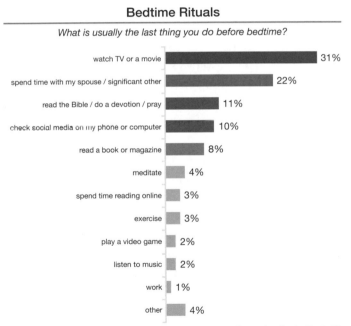

Bedtime Rituals

What is usually the last thing you do before bedtime?

- watch TV or a movie — 31%
- spend time with my spouse / significant other — 22%
- read the Bible / do a devotion / pray — 11%
- check social media on my phone or computer — 10%
- read a book or magazine — 8%
- meditate — 4%
- spend time reading online — 3%
- exercise — 3%
- play a video game — 2%
- listen to music — 2%
- work — 1%
- other — 4%

n = 1,021 US parents of children ages 4 to 17; due to rounding, numbers do not add up to 100

is especially bad for sleep, fooling our bodies into thinking that it is still daylight.[2] (I use third-party programs like f.lux and Apple's own settings to make sure my devices glow yellow rather than blue at night.) Either way, screens also interrupt our sleep by bringing before us the constant stream of entertainment, titillation, communication, and demands of our daytime lives.

The problem is especially acute for the emerging generation—our kids—who depend on messaging apps for most social engagement. The messages stream in day and night and deep into the wee hours of the morning. (Somebody liked my Instagram photo! I have a message from a friend! Someone commented on my post! I was added to a group text!) These messages are full of the positive reinforcement we all crave, whatever our age, and the social signals of disapproval and shame we all fear.

The nighttime bedroom also lends itself to disinhibition and foolish choices—such as consuming images with sexual content and, disturbingly often for teens, especially teen girls, making those images for the satisfaction of others. (Even the most robust internet filter on a home network or a child's phone does nothing to filter pictures sent via messaging applications.) In person and with a good night's sleep, almost all of us would be far more careful with our own bodies and would exercise better judgment over the flights of our own imaginations than we do late at night. Fatigue and isolation compound our immaturity and susceptibility to temptation—especially for teenagers but also for adults. (This is why it's so alarming that more than eight in ten parents say their teenagers have their phones with them when they sleep; among the parents themselves, seven in ten sleep with their phones next to the bed.)[3]

And even at their best, social media, like all media, substitute distant relationships for close ones. A fifteen-year-old overcome by anxiety late at night might once have had no choice but to turn to her parents, down the hall from her bedroom, for help and counsel. Now she can send out a blizzard of text messages to friends who, completely understandably, feel obligated to respond—and feel gratified by the sense of being needed by a friend. But this text- and emoji-mediated social support is thin, an echo chamber of teenagers with their limited perspective. It keeps a whole circle of friends awake late into the night and robs that fifteen-year-old and her parents (or even older siblings) of an in-person conversation, one that could be painful, challenging, reassuring, or even transformative.

Under the covers, as alerts light up the night, anxieties and fantasies are fed as often as they are allayed—for parents as much as children. And we lose out on what we were really made for: the deep rest that would make us more cognitively, emotionally, physically, and spiritually fit for the challenges the next day will bring. The lilies of the field close up their blooms at night and rest patiently for the next day, but we, cloaked in ghostly light, make tomorrow's troubles today's and tonight's instead. The devices we carry to bed to make us feel connected and safe actually prevent us from trusting in the One who knows our needs and who alone can protect us through the dangers and sorrows of any night.

Sweet Dreams, Little Smartphone

So, we need a simple discipline: our devices should "go to bed" before we do. And to add a nudge to that discipline, it's by far the best if their "bedroom" is as far from ours as possible. It may be that one adult, at least, needs a phone nearby at night in case of emergency, but most children and teenagers (and, um, dads) lack the self-discipline to turn their smartphones to "Do Not Disturb" and put them facedown on the bedside table for a solid eight or nine hours.

So find a central place in the home, far from the bedrooms, and park the screens there before bedtime. (All this applies, a thousand times over, to the glowing overstimulation of television—surely the single least helpful thing, short of a jackhammer, you could ever put in a place where someone is trying to fall asleep. In fact, most television programming, designed to catch and keep the attention of a distracted public, is the visual equivalent of a jackhammer.) Buy a cheap alarm clock so you don't have to rely on a smartphone to wake you up. Sleep specialists widely recommend that, once night comes, the bedroom should be reserved for just one thing: sleep (and, for the parents, romance). Make it so.

In the interval between putting the devices to bed and laying your own head on the pillow, spend a few minutes in the darkening quiet talking, praying, or reading by the calming reflected light from a page.

And then, in the morning, rather than rolling over to check for whatever flotsam and jetsam arrived in the night, get up

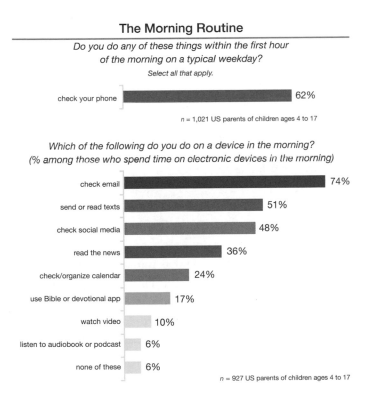

The Morning Routine

Do you do any of these things within the first hour of the morning on a typical weekday?

Select all that apply.

check your phone — 62%

n = 1,021 US parents of children ages 4 to 17

Which of the following do you do on a device in the morning?
(% among those who spend time on electronic devices in the morning)

check email — 74%
send or read texts — 51%
check social media — 48%
read the news — 36%
check/organize calendar — 24%
use Bible or devotional app — 17%
watch video — 10%
listen to audiobook or podcast — 6%
none of these — 6%

n = 927 US parents of children ages 4 to 17

The most common way Americans end their day is to watch television or a movie (31%) or spend time with their spouse / significant other (22%). Some people read the Bible (11%); a few meditate (4%). Fewer than one in ten (8%) read a book or magazine before bed. And only one in ten say they check social media before bed. But when they do go to bed, most people take their phones with them. A full seven in ten parents say they sleep with their phone next to them. Alarmingly, parents say their kids are even more likely to take their phones to bed: more than eight in ten parents of teens (82%) say their child takes their phone to bed and more than seven in ten parents of preteens (72%) say the same. And when that phone is right next to you, it's tempting to reach for it when you wake up: 62 percent of parents say checking their phone is one of the first things they do in the morning. What are they doing on their phone while they rub away the cobwebs of sleep? Most check their email (74%). Social media (48%), news (36%), and calendar organization (24%) also vie for their attention. Less than one in five (17%) are using a Bible or devotional app.

and do something—anything—before plugging in. Stretch. Shower. Open the front door for a moment and breathe the morning's air, humid or frigid as it may be. Make coffee or tea and wait for the brew to finish. There is something for you to discover in these moments just after waking that you will never know if you rush past it—an almost-forgotten dream, a secret fear, a spark of something creative. You'll have the rest of the day tethered to the impatient wider world; let that wait a moment. Give your devices one more minute in their "beds." Practice the grateful breath of someone who slept and awakened, given the gift of one more day.

You slept and allowed God to be enough. Now, for at least a moment, wake and be still, letting him be enough for this day. Then you can say good morning to whatever the day brings.

Crouch Family
Reality Check

We've been wildly inconsistent here. Our attempts to enforce the common bedtime (and "bedroom") for devices have been met with stubborn resistance from our teenagers. And it's easy for the parents to carry our little screens with us up to bed, letting them entertain us during the routine of flossing and brushing and face washing. Our children swear they set their devices on "Do Not Disturb" and sleep undisturbed—maybe they are even telling us the truth.

As for the mornings—oh, how far many of my mornings are from the best kind of beginning to the day. I scroll through notifications while the tea is still brewing. Before I've even fully woken up, I submit myself to whatever random acts of outrage have been catalogued and stored up for me overnight. Catherine and our kids are better at this than I am, less likely to download a full day's worth of detritus before the day has even started.

So this chapter is one that the Crouches are far from fulfilling. But I happen to have friends who keep every single word of this chapter as a married couple and as a family, after some harrowing encounters with the dangers of constant access to screens and all their temptations. Their devices sleep long and do so far from their beds. They are the sanest people I know—far saner and healthier than we are. We need what they have.

5

Learning and Working

5. We aim for "no screens before double digits" at school and at home.

Human beings are bodies. This is much truer than saying we "have" bodies—as if we could do without them or leave them behind. We are also souls—unique and irreplaceable selves that exist in and beyond our physical nature. We don't "have" souls any more than we "have" bodies. We are both, soul and body together, and the Christian faith, rooted in ancient Hebrew belief, teaches that they were always meant to go together and, thanks to the resurrection of the body, always will.

These convictions, that being human involves both body and soul and that both body and soul will somehow outlast even death, are certainly not universal. Whole civilizations and religions have believed that human beings are only "really" souls, with our bodies an awkward and temporary prison. More recently, some secular modernists believe we are only "really" bodies, with no such thing as a soul.

But the further we explore into the astonishingly complex nature of human beings, especially the mysterious bodily organ called the "brain" and the even more mysterious reality of personhood called the "mind," the more the Hebrew perspective seems fundamentally sound. And nowhere is it more evident that we are body and soul together than in studies of how we *learn*.

The best and richest experiences of learning, it turns out, are embodied ones. They require and build on physical experience and activity. This begins with the most basic things typical children learn in their first years of life. (Even those who are not cognitively or developmentally typical follow at least part of this path.) They learn, beautifully, awkwardly, and sometimes hilariously, all the aspects of living in a body: crawling and walking, eating and feeding oneself, and let's not forget the most rewarding for parents, toilet training! And they also learn that most extraordinary human ability, language.

With little effort and much delight, typical human children master the essentials of an entire language—their "mother tongue"—by the time they are four or five years old. And this is an entirely embodied affair. The word *language* itself comes from the Latin root for *tongue*. We learn language not by being taught abstract concepts of language but by using our tongue, teeth, lungs, and vocal chords to produce sound. (Deaf children who learn to sign use hands, arms, and facial expressions in the same embodied way.) And then when, later on, we learn to read, we begin by "sounding out" the symbols on the page. We learn through our bodies' active engagement with sound and sight. Even if, like the famous American educator Helen Keller, we are robbed of both sound and sight early in our lives, we can learn, as she did, through touch.

As we go on to learn more complex and abstract things, the body continues to play an important role. At the most basic level, everything we learn is encoded in chemical and electrical connections between neurons in our brains—the physical connections that are solidified and strengthened during sleep, as discussed in the previous chapter. But our bodies play a part during the waking hours as well. Cognitive scientists like Maryanne Wolf, author of *Proust and the Squid: The Story and Science of the Reading Brain*, and Abigail Sellen, a principal researcher for Microsoft who coauthored a book called *The Myth of the Paperless Office*, observe that the physical act of reading a book, with its bound pages, helps strengthen the learning of the concepts inside.[1] (If you are reading this book in physical form, you may well be able to remember, hours or days from now, where on the page and how far into the book this very sentence was found—a physical memory of your senses from eyes and hands that will reinforce the idea you absorbed at the same time. That experience will be missing if you read it on a digital screen, with no fixed location on a page, no weight of the two halves of the book in your hands, and the idea itself will also be harder to remember.)

Likewise, physically taking notes with a pen or pencil on paper—the act of forming physical letters by hand, with the twists and turns of the letter forms and the accumulating fatigue and need for rest—turns out to aid memorization and learning, *even if we never consult the notes again*. Other bodily activities help us learn as well—making up songs and rhymes that we chant to ourselves to remember otherwise obscure sequences of concepts ("King Philip Came Over For Good Soup," biology students may repeat aloud, and their brains will conjure up images of crowned monarchs and the savor of hot broth even as they also remember the sequence of kingdom, phylum, class, order, family, genus, and species). Physical activity engages our brains in ways that mere thought or contemplation does not—indeed, there is reason to believe there is no such thing as "mere thought." All human thought requires embodiment, and without bodies we could not think. We can have a faint idea or hunch in our mind, but it is only when we speak or write it that it becomes clear, not just to others but to ourselves as well.

We are made to live and learn in a physical world. And no human beings are more exuberantly and fundamentally rooted in the body than children. As children, our bodies are full of energy and primed for physical learning. We are designed to explore our world and learn through all our senses.

So it could be that the proliferation of technology, especially screens, at earlier and earlier ages, may well be remembered as one of the most damaging epidemics of the twenty-first century.

Dangerously Easy

The last thing you need when you are learning, at any age but especially in childhood, is to have things made too easy. Difficulty and resistance, as long as they are age appropriate and not too discouraging, are actually what press our brains and bodies to adapt and learn. From the earliest games of peekaboo to the challenge of mastering a sport or a musical instrument, we are designed to thrive on complex, embodied tasks that require the engagement of many senses at once, and not just our senses but our muscles, from the tiny adjustments possible in the human hand or voice to the gross motor movements of legs and arms. Even something as seemingly inactive as reading a book involves not just our eyes but our hands, which help us learn as they handle the book's weight and the changing balance of its pages.

But now, very early on in our lives and learning, we are substituting a single kind of activity, a dangerously easy and simple one, for the difficult, multidimensional kinds of activity that the real world offers us. We hand our children screen-based devices that, at this writing at least, respond to only a few very simple kinds of touch. They are exquisitely engineered to be easy to use, and their screens glow in colors

Time and Limits on Devices

How many hours do your children spend using an electronic device (tablet, phone, computer) on a typical weekday?

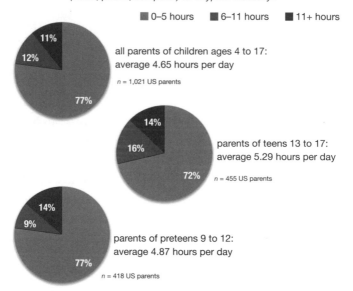

■ 0–5 hours   ■ 6–11 hours   ■ 11+ hours

all parents of children ages 4 to 17: average 4.65 hours per day

n = 1,021 US parents

parents of teens 13 to 17: average 5.29 hours per day

n = 455 US parents

parents of preteens 9 to 12: average 4.87 hours per day

n = 418 US parents

far brighter than we almost ever see in nature. No wonder they are so enticing to children. And it's neither surprising nor impressive that our children figure them out so quickly.

The biggest problem with most screen-based activities is that because they are designed to keep us engaged, we can learn them far too quickly. They ask too little of us and make the world too simple. To learn to play an acoustic guitar requires hundreds of hours of practice involving physical

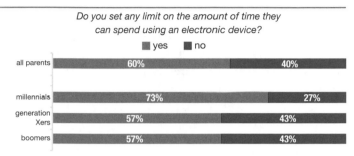

Do you set any limit on the amount of time they can spend using an electronic device?

■ yes ■ no

all parents	60%	40%
millennials	73%	27%
generation Xers	57%	43%
boomers	57%	43%

n = 960 US parents of children ages 4 to 17 whose children spend time using electronic devices on a typical day

strength and stamina, the development of calluses on the hand (usually the left) that holds down the strings, the ability to hear tiny variations of tone and timbre as we pluck and strum at different speeds and angles and to adjust our movements accordingly. A "guitar app," on the other hand, vastly oversimplifies all these dimensions of embodied music making, replacing them with a skill that is far more easily acquired and requires far less learning.

And this might be totally fine—as *leisure*. But our first years on this planet are the time when we can be *learning*, when we are primed to learn in embodied ways. There is a whole amazing world to explore that requires body and soul together. And increasingly, instead of spending their days playing and learning in that rich, complex, demanding world, our children are engaging in the same kind of limited, limiting game-like activity that adults engage in to pass the time on their daily commutes. When our children could be making candy (learning about the different phases of sugar as it heats from soft ball to hard crack, the glories of caramelization, the bitterness of burnt sugar—all the possibilities and dangers of heat), they are playing Candy Crush.

Difficult and Rewarding

Of course, making candy, or many other demanding activities, requires the involvement of parents, other responsible adults, or perhaps older siblings. (We most often give our children screens not to make their lives easier but to make *our* lives easier.) But even in the place where adults are specifically charged with helping children learn—in school—the easy-everywhere promises of technology are taking over.

There is one common justification for the early introduction of technology into school classrooms—that children need to become "computer literate," as if learning to use computers were somehow as difficult and rewarding as learning to read itself. But this is a massively confused idea. The "computers" used in far too many classrooms in the United States are incredibly *easy* to use—more and more so as they approach technology's ultimate promise of easy everywhere. A three-year-old (or a ninety-three-year-old) can intuitively figure out how to use an iPad. There is almost nothing to teach, and certainly nothing that any typical person can't learn with a few hours of practice.

Now, the actual work of programming computers is indeed a wonderful form of creative literacy, just as beautiful as mathematics or poetry—a worthy use of a lifetime of learning and creating. But that is not what is being taught when third graders are asked to make a PowerPoint presentation or play an "educational game." Instead, their precious time and prodigious capacity for developing bodily skill is being diverted into thin, superficially rewarding activities far less demanding than creating a real poster with foam core and markers or playing a real game on the playground.

The truth is that our children, just like us, will spend far too much of their lives tethered to glowing rectangles. We owe them, at the very minimum, early years of real, embodied, difficult, rewarding learning, the kind that screens cannot provide. And that is why a family that cares about developing wisdom and courage will exert every effort to avoid the thin simplicity of screens in the first years of life. Our family adopted a simple if radical standard: *no screens before double digits.* Until our children were ten years old, screens just weren't a regular part of their lives.

Of course, there's nothing magical about the tenth birthday. But it's a convenient marker and a worthy goal. And really, is ten solid years spent in the real, three-dimensional world too much to ask? If anything, ten years are too few.

I realize that for many readers of this book, this will sound impossible. In a strict sense, it *is* impossible for any family in urban and suburban America—screens have colonized many public spaces, and even ordering a sandwich at our local convenience store requires using a touch screen. Not to mention that when our son was between eight and twelve years old, the social life of boys seemed to revolve almost exclusively around video games, which made playdates at our home boring for them and awkward for him and for us.

So legalism in this area, like any other, is unwise and unhelpful. But we can still radically limit the amount of time our children spend directly engaging with screens in their youngest years. First, eliminate "passive" screen time at home—televisions or videos playing in the background with no one even really paying attention. Then reduce or eliminate "unaccompanied" screen time—the games and videos that substitute for individual play and reading. Then take the more challenging step of reducing "social" screen time, figuring out how to challenge children to play together in tactile, creative, self-initiated, and self-sustaining ways. Our family also eliminated advertising-supported television entirely with the simple step of not buying a TV until our children were in double digits. And even then, only very occasionally, perhaps once a month, would we watch an intentionally chosen movie together.

Just making these choices at home will have a beneficial effect, even if we recognize that our children will get all too much screen time at friends' homes and at school. But there is no doubt that making this commitment requires creativity, energy, and patience from parents as well as children.

Still, I have encountered numerous encouraging examples of families who changed course midway through their children's early years, discarding the TV and radically limiting other forms of screen-based entertainment. They testify that the withdrawal process was excruciating, but that a month later, let alone a year later, everyone in the family was far happier, more engaged with one another, and less bored. As I'll discuss in the next chapter, the quest to cure boredom with entertainment actually makes the problem worse. But it works the other way around as well. The less we rely on screens to occupy and entertain our children, the more they become capable of occupying and entertaining themselves.

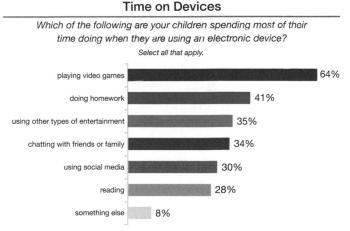

Time on Devices

Which of the following are your children spending most of their time doing when they are using an electronic device?

Select all that apply.

- playing video games — 64%
- doing homework — 41%
- using other types of entertainment — 35%
- chatting with friends or family — 34%
- using social media — 30%
- reading — 28%
- something else — 8%

n = 960 US parents of children ages 4 to 17 whose children spend time using electronic devices on a typical day

Ultimately this kind of commitment requires community and advocacy. It helps tremendously if even a few other families take the same basic approach to play and life at home. It's even better if a whole church community can make a screen-free life for their children the rule rather than the exception. And a few families who advocate with teachers, principals, and school boards can make a huge difference in helping change approaches to elementary education.

There is no reason to think this will impair our children's learning in the least. All of our modern wonders of science and technology, after all—not to mention the world's treasures of literature and poetry, songs and dance, sports and cuisine—were created by men and women whose childhoods were free of screens. And a ten- or eleven-year-old can figure out an iPad (or whatever has replaced it by the time she turns that age) in an instant. By that age, as well, she will begin to be cognitively ready to actually become "computer literate"—to be taught and to practice the fascinating algorithmic and mathematical thinking that is at the heart of much technology. And she will have had a real childhood, with dirt under her fingernails, countless books nearly memorized through delighted rereading, and complex, embodied skills encoded into her still-growing brain. She will enjoy the rich life of a soul in a body, rather than being reduced to a brain on a stick.

This is one of the greatest, most radical gifts we can give our children: ten years free to be embodied human beings, before we begin helping them manage the complexities as well as the gifts of the screen-based world. Give them those ten years, and I believe many of the patterns that are overwhelming parents as well as teenagers and young adults—let alone the frustrations that teachers are experiencing with ever-declining attention spans and capacity to concentrate—will be far more manageable.

What applies to children can apply to us adults as well. Many of us spend most of our working hours tethered to screens—such is the power and value of these tools for representing the world and working with others. But we can attend to the needs and possibilities of our bodies too. I do most of my writing, almost all of which requires a screen, in twenty-four-minute intervals, punctuated by six- to thirty-minute rest periods that give me a chance to weed the garden, walk around the block, brew tea, wash dishes, practice a page of Bach, or otherwise engage my full body. Our screen-based work will be far more productive if we balance it with plunges back into the complex, three-dimensional physical world that reawakens both our brains and our minds, both our bodies and our souls.[2]

Swimming Upstream

Many of the core commitments in this book are counter-cultural, at the very least. This one requires us to swim especially hard against the cultural flow. The sad truth is that many schools are intoxicated with technology, for which they can apply for scarce and precious grant money, and intimidated by suggestions that their students might end up "behind" others if they don't start manipulating tablets and trackpads early enough. Parents who want their schools to choose another way will likely find themselves arguing not so much with actual research about the educational benefits of technology in elementary school as with vague platitudes about "moving education into the twenty-first century."

Choosing no screens before double digits at home, and advocating for the same at school, is hard. Screens are easy. Screens are engrossing, absorbing, and rewarding for children just as much as for adults. If our goal is to have engrossed, absorbed, and easily rewarded children, we will turn to screens every time. And there are certain situations—for example, the

Who Has a Phone?

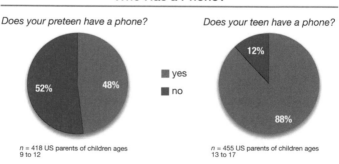

Does your preteen have a phone?

52% | 48%

■ yes
■ no

n = 418 US parents of children ages 9 to 12

Does your teen have a phone?

12%

88%

n = 455 US parents of children ages 13 to 17

Children are spending an average of five hours on an electronic device (tablet, phone, computer, etc.) every day. Their most common activity? Playing video games. Nearly two-thirds of parents say their children spend most of their time on an electronic device playing video games (64%), compared to four in ten who mostly do homework (41%), one-third who are using other types of entertainment (35%), and one-third who are chatting with friends or family (34%). About three in ten are either using social media (30%) or reading (28%). Even at five hours a day, most parents say they are limiting the amount of time their kids spend on electronic devices (60%). Millennial parents—perhaps because they have younger children or perhaps because they are more likely to be immersed in and therefore experiencing their own angst around electronic usage—are more likely (73%) than generation Xer (57%) or boomer parents (57%) to limit their children's time on electronic devices. Limiting time seems more popular than eliminating the devices: most kids have phones. Nearly nine in ten parents with teenagers (88%) say their teen has a phone and just under half of parents with preteens (48%) say their child does.

encouraging ways that technology is assisting autistic children and their families to communicate—where screens and other devices are wonderfully useful.[3] But for most kinds of learning, developing children's minds and hearts with a deep connection to their bodies and the world around them, we'll have to choose the more excellent way—glowing-rectangle free.

That, of course, will require us to deal with our children's complaints—and our own—that a life without screens is too boring to bear. And that is the subject of the next chapter.

. . . . Crouch Family . . . .
Reality Check

With a few exceptions, we managed to live out this commitment when our own children were in single digits. As I mentioned above, we held off on buying a television, that massive nudge toward screen-based entertainment, until our youngest child was ten years old. And we were fortunate to live in a school district that did not overemphasize technology in the early elementary grades.

We made a few exceptions. Our son showed early interest in computers, and we let him learn to type using a computer-based instructional program when he was quite young. Our children certainly looked over our shoulders countless times as we consulted Wikipedia for the answer to questions about science or history. And for the several years when I taught our daughter Latin, screen-based exercises were valuable for both her and me.

But mostly our children (who are now, like all teenagers, more adept than we really want to know in the ways of technology) spent their single-digit years learning in a world full of things, complicated things in three dimensions, not a world full of devices, simplified if beautiful illusions in two dimensions. They now say they wouldn't want it any other way.

6

....

The Good News about Boredom

> 6. We use screens for a purpose, and we use them together,
> rather than using them aimlessly and alone.

In the history of the human race, boredom is practically brand
new—less than three hundred years old.

The English word does not appear until the 1850s, and its
parent word *bore* (as a noun—"he is such a bore") appears
only a century earlier. The French word *ennui* begins to mean
what we call "boredom" around the same time.[1] Before the
eighteenth century, there simply wasn't a common word for
that feeling of frustration and lassitude that overtakes so
many of us so often—not just in long lines at the grocery
store or the airport but in our own homes as well.

Could it be that modern life is boring in a way that pre-
modern life was not? How could this be? Our world has more

Time and Limits on TV

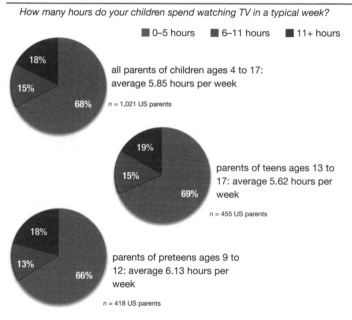

How many hours do your children spend watching TV in a typical week?

■ 0–5 hours   ■ 6–11 hours   ■ 11+ hours

all parents of children ages 4 to 17:
average 5.85 hours per week

n = 1,021 US parents

parents of teens ages 13 to
17: average 5.62 hours per
week

n = 455 US parents

parents of preteens ages 9 to
12: average 6.13 hours per
week

n = 418 US parents

distractions and entertainments than we can ever consume. We feel busy and overworked in ways even our grandparents couldn't have imagined (even as many of us work far less hard, physically, than most of them did).

But that's actually *why* we get bored. Boredom—for children and for adults—is a perfectly modern condition. The technology that promises to release us from boredom is actually making it worse—making us more prone to seek

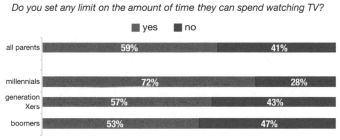

Do you set any limit on the amount of time they can spend watching TV?

■ yes   ■ no

all parents	59%	41%
millennials	72%	28%
generation Xers	57%	43%
boomers	53%	47%

n = 991 US parents of children ages 4 to 17 whose children watch TV on a typical weekday

empty distractions than we have ever been. In fact, I've come to the conclusion that *the more you entertain children, the more bored they will get.*

This may seem totally wrong to any parent who has been desperate to quiet down restless young children. Put on a brightly colored, fast-moving video, and your kids will stay slack-jawed and motionless for the half hour it takes to get dinner on the table. (Is there any half hour more stressful in more homes than the one right before dinner? Friends of mine with three young children used to call it "the witching hour," which is probably unfair to actual witches.) What could possibly be wrong with something that solves such an urgent problem so neatly?

The problem, as with so many short-term solutions, is that solving the immediate problem requires leaving a bigger problem unsolved—and actually makes the bigger problem worse.

How Videos Bewitch

The truth is that the real "bewitching" doesn't happen when our kids are going half crazy with hunger and pent-up end-of-the-day energy and parents are feeling all the accumulated frustrations of the day. It happens at many moments when we give ourselves over to technological entertainment.

Because make no mistake: the videos we put on for our kids—or the video games we pull up on our phones in our own moments of boredom—are designed, unconsciously or consciously, to produce a bewitching effect. And that effect is achieved by filling a screen with a level of vividness and velocity that does not exist in the real world—or only very rarely. Because it is rare, we instinctively respond to it, and indeed take delight in it.

In my backyard, with its mottled shades of green, suddenly I spot a cardinal flitting from one tree to another. He is vivid red and gone in a flash. If I hadn't been gazing out the window, I would have missed him. During a moonless night, a meteor suddenly streaks across the sky, just barely catching the corner of my vision. Only by lying on my back for minutes or hours did I make myself available to see that brilliance.

But the entertainment we serve up to our children, and ourselves, constantly fills the screen with movement as swift as the meteor's and colors as brilliant as the cardinal's. It is purposefully edited to never require too much concentration or contemplation; instead, it grabs our attention and constantly stimulates our desire and delight in novelty. But in doing so, it gradually desensitizes us as well.

Watching movies or TV shows from the early days of moving pictures reminds us of just how frantic this attention-holding game has become. In the early days, cameras could stay still and on-screen subjects could utter whole paragraphs of dialogue. Now cuts get faster and faster; colors get more and more saturated. Keeping us entertained is getting harder and harder. We are bored far more easily than we once were.

The same is true in thoroughly adult entertainment. Twenty years ago *The Sopranos* was a critical favorite and audience hit in part because of its boundary-pushing depictions of sex and violence, along with its intricate plots of jealousy, loyalty, and betrayal. As I write, the hit show of the moment is *Game of Thrones*, whose levels of psychological drama, not to mention lurid sex, violence, and violent sex, make *The Sopranos* look like something from an age of innocence. A world in which *The Sopranos* can seem innocent is a world ratcheting its way toward being unable to be shocked by anything—which is to say, a world completely full of boredom.

As screens—movies, TV, video games—present a world far more colorful and energetic than the created world itself, they not only ratchet up our expectations for what is significant and entertaining; they also undermine our ability to enjoy what we could call *the abundance of the ordinary*. Even when there is no cardinal in my backyard, it is full of varied colors, shapes, and sounds: the rustle of the breeze in the bushes, the subtly different leaves and bark of oak and maple, the infinite varieties of green against the changing sky. Even when there is no meteor shower, the night sky's stars and nebulae are of countless different brightnesses and even shades of color, and they shimmer in the air. They form constellations in our ancestors' imaginations and our own. Seeing a cardinal or a meteor is a special event, but in fact the very ordinary analog world is itself charged with beauty and surprise.

And the ones who used to be able to see this ordinary abundance in all its glory, in all its full capacity to delight and transfix our attention, were children. Children were the ones who simply went out to play in the ordinary world, even with no toys at all, because they had something far better than toys: grass and dirt, worms and beetles, trees and fields. The world they played in was rich, substantial, and rewarding of attention: the closer you looked, the more you saw; the more you listened, the more you heard.

This world is lost to many of our children, and to ourselves. Even the "nature" that surrounds many of our homes is shallow in a technological way. A typical suburban lawn depends on many technological devices, each of which makes something far easier than it was for previous generations: lawn mowers, pesticides and fertilizers, highly refined seed, and automatic sprinklers. The lawn itself is a kind of outdoor technological device, composed of uniform green grass, kept crew-cut short, with little variety or difference.

A peasant family in the Middle Ages had none of this technologically uniform pleasantness. They would not have had a lawn, or possibly even a yard. Their children would have wandered out into meadows and perhaps the thin edges of forests. A meadow has countless different species of grasses and other plants, plus flowers in the spring and summer, of different heights and habits. If you pay attention, you cannot possibly get bored in a meadow. It is all too easy to be bored on a lawn.

So here is one result of our technology: we become people who desperately need entertainment and distraction because we have lost the world of meadows and meteors. Quite literally *lost*—where can my own children go to see a meadow? How far from the city would we have to drive for them to see a meteor in the night sky? But very nearby are technological forms of distraction, from video games to constantly updated social media. They do little to develop our abilities to wait, pay attention, contemplate, and explore—all needed to discover the abundance of the ordinary.

It is surely not coincidental that all the earliest citations of the word *bore* in the Oxford English Dictionary—from the mid-eighteenth century—come from the correspondence of aristocrats and nobility.[2] They did not have technology, but thanks to wealth and position they had a kind of easy everywhere of their own. The first people to be bored were the people who did not do manual work, who did not cook their own food, whose lives were served by others. They were also, by the way, the very first people to have lawns.[3]

Distraction and Delight

Boredom is actually a crucial warning sign—as important in its own way as physical pain. It's a sign that our capacity for wonder and delight, contemplation and attention, real play and fruitful work, has been dangerously depleted.

Boredom may have peaked at the height of the industrial age, as children sat in mechanical rows of desks at school and adults were slotted into assembly-line rows, whether in blue-collar factories or white-collar offices, reduced to cogs in an industrial machine. But there is a new challenge in our postindustrial times, with vast amounts of computing power channeled into screens we carry everywhere. We now have the technology to be perpetually distracted from boredom, and thus we never realize how bored we really are.

Standing in every line you will see people thumbing through an infinite scroll of messages, images, news stories, and posts on their glowing rectangles. They are waiting in environments that, if they were not so familiar, we would recognize are indeed brutally dull: either, like most airport lines, devoid of any hint of the complexity and beauty of the organic world or, like most grocery store lines, numbingly overstuffed with packaging and commercial messages. So we all turn to our array of apps for relief (Facebook for the olds, Snapchat for the not-so-olds, something whose name I don't know yet for the fourteen-year-olds). We are not bored, exactly, just as someone eating potato chips is not hungry, exactly. But overconsumption of distraction is just as unsatisfying, and ultimately sickening, as overconsumption of junk food.

You probably wouldn't be reading this book if you hadn't had at least a few times in your life when you were thoroughly unbored—by a good story, a long walk, or an absorbing piece of music. At the end you felt alive, refreshed, and alert. But you probably wouldn't be reading this book if you hadn't also spent an hour being distracted from boredom by the "junk feeds" on your phone—and at the end just felt disoriented and spent.

This is why our short-term solution to the witching hour—to bewitch our children with technological distraction—in the long run just makes things worse. And as with all the things we do to our children, the truth is that we are doing it to ourselves as well. I am horrified at the hours I have spent, often in the face of demanding creative work, scrolling aimlessly through social media and news updates, clicking briefly on countless vaguely titillating updates about people I barely know and situations I have no control over, feeling dim, thin versions of interest, attraction, dissatisfaction, and dislike. Those hours have been spent avoiding suffering—avoiding the suffering of our banal, boring modern world with its airport security lines and traffic jams and parking lots, but also avoiding the suffering of learning patience, wisdom, and virtue and putting them into practice. They have left me, as the ring left Bilbo, feeling "all thin, sort of *stretched*, if you know what I mean: like butter that has been scraped over too much bread."[4]

Weeknight Plans

On a typical weeknight, how do your children generally spend their time?
Select all that apply.

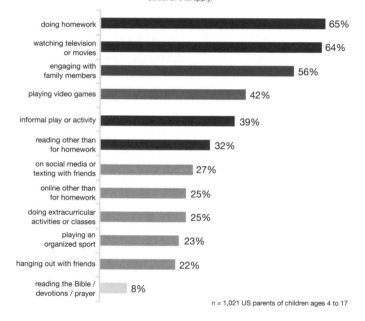

doing homework	65%
watching television or movies	64%
engaging with family members	56%
playing video games	42%
informal play or activity	39%
reading other than for homework	32%
on social media or texting with friends	27%
online other than for homework	25%
doing extracurricular activities or classes	25%
playing an organized sport	23%
hanging out with friends	22%
reading the Bible / devotions / prayer	8%

n = 1,021 US parents of children ages 4 to 17

Screens on Purpose

As with so much in our mediated world, the solution to this mess is astonishingly simple, and radical only because it is so rarely done. The problem isn't with our devices themselves—it's with the way we use them. We simply have to turn off the easy fixes and make media something we use on purpose and rarely rather than aimlessly and frequently.

So when we do sit down in front of a TV screen, it will be for a specific purpose and with a specific hope, not just of entertainment or distraction but of wonder and exploration. When we do scroll through social media, it will be to have a chance to give thanks for our friends, enjoy their creative gifts, and pray for their needs, rather than just something to take our mind off our tedium.

And this means that most of the time, the screens stay blank. We will never, ever figure out how to help our children—and ourselves—survive that maddening half hour before dinner if we always settle for the screen. Instead, we will simply decide that whatever else happens in those confounding moments of children's boredom and parents' frustration, we will find some solution other than mediated entertainment.

The good news is that the more often we resist the easy solution, the easier the solution will be to find—because our children (and we ourselves) will start to develop capacities to explore and discover that will make them less prone to be bored in the first place. The discipline here is committing to this simple rule: the screen stays off and blank unless we are using it together and for a specific creative purpose. Then we can put nudges in place. If the craft table is always set up and within earshot of the kitchen, 5:30 p.m. is an ideal time to get out the watercolors or the finger paints (our craft table was designed to be stainproof and waterproof, but an

149

Family Time

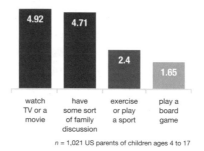

*In the past two weeks, how many times did your
family do any of the following together?*

Mean average among all parents.

4.92	4.71	2.4	1.65
watch TV or a movie	have some sort of family discussion	exercise or play a sport	play a board game

n = 1,021 US parents of children ages 4 to 17

equally good solution is to have an old table devoted to total mayhem, with a rubberized picnic tablecloth underfoot).

And when we do put on a video or otherwise fire up a screen for a purpose, we'll follow another principle: never entertain your children with anything you find unsatisfying, just like you shouldn't feed your children anything you don't enjoy eating yourself. Feed them with food that is both tasty and nutritious—and entertain them with movies, books, and stories that are both tasty and nutritious too.

This doesn't mean avoiding all "children's" movies or books (or food). It just means avoiding the ones that are too simple or simplistic to satisfy adults. Plenty of children's entertainment passes the adults-too test. My wife and I still recite passages aloud to one another from the Dr. Seuss books

Watching television is still a favorite American pastime. Aside from doing homework (65%), it is the activity parents say their children are most likely to be engaged in after school (64%). And it is the activity families do together most frequently (compared to having family discussions, playing board games, and playing sports). Aside from television watching, technology occupies a central place in many of the after-school activities of children: four in ten parents (42%) say their children regularly play video games after school, three in ten (27%) are on social media or texting with friends, and a quarter (25%) are online other than for homework. Of course, there's plenty of off-line activity too: nearly six in ten (56%) spend time engaging with family members, four in ten (39%) are playing informally, one-third (32%) are reading other than for homework, a quarter (23%) are playing organized sports, and more than one-fifth (22%) are hanging out with friends.

we read to our small children; they may be doggerel, but they are endlessly inventive and delightful. One of the great virtues of the movie studio Pixar is that almost all its films have enough complexity, texture, intelligence, and heart to be fully and deeply enjoyed by adults. There are many "children's Bibles" that I find saccharine sweet and would never have let near my own kids, but Sally Lloyd-Jones's best-selling *Jesus Storybook Bible* is surprising and moving, with its artful words and graceful art, every time I open it to a random page.[5]

The fact is that even our world diminished by technology is still stuffed with wonder. There *is* a meadow within a short drive of our home, and we've sometimes driven an hour or more to get to a place with a sky dark enough to see a meteor shower. There are movies that repay our attention, books worth reading when we are ten years old and rereading every ten years until old age. Give a child watercolors or finger paints and enough time and sheets of paper, and she will one day paint something that will be worth framing and keeping on your wall for the rest of your life. The lawn outside may be no meadow, but you can still find worms and beetles if you look carefully, and you can spot the occasional cardinal.

We will stay indoors some days and evenings, yes, and enjoy the best art and entertainment that our astonishingly creative fellow human beings have created—but by enjoying the best, on purpose, rarely and together, we'll become the kind of people who can also find the best in anything, wherever we are, even alone. We'll become the kind of people who can never be bored.

Crouch Family
Reality Check

I can say with little hesitation that by severely limiting our children's access to screens and mediated entertainment, we gave them this kind of childhood: one grounded in the beautifully simple and endlessly complex created world.

But my own life has been more and more infested by distraction and shallowness over the last ten to twenty years. My life has a toxic combination of two things: a great deal of time in tedious settings like airports, and a great deal of freedom, the free time that is necessary for the creative calling of a writer and musician. In both of these settings, seemingly so opposite from one another—the grim sameness of travel and the blissful silence and open hours of a writer's daily schedule—I have been sucked into the most trivial forms of distraction.

In this, as with so many things in this book, the biggest problem was not the kids—it was the dad.

7

The Deep End
of the (Car) Pool

What would you say if I told you there was a place where you could talk with kids—really talk— about everything that truly matters: relationships, faith, school, the future, the past? Where conversations would last long enough to get beyond both superficiality and awkward silence to the deep truth and to real silence as well, the kind of silence that holds and bears both joy and pain?

I would never have expected the place where our family most often has found that kind of conversation. It was, actually, the place I most dreaded as I anticipated being a parent, especially of middle school and high school kids.

155

It was the car.

As our children left elementary school—which for our family meant leaving the school just a five-minute walk away, with its wonderfully small circle of neighborhood relationships—I anticipated years of tedious car trips to sports events, musical rehearsals, and friends' houses.

Now, near the end of our children's high school years, I can truly say that some of the most treasured and transforming conversations I have had with each of our children came on routine trips—which were, indeed, just as numerous and in some ways tedious as I had expected. As I write this chapter, our daughter has just qualified for her learner's permit to drive, and I find myself oddly wistful at the thought of her driving herself to all those events, with no more need for her dad or mom to chauffeur. One dad whose children have already passed that threshold said to me, "I thought I would miss them when they went off to college, but I realized that the bigger loss came sooner, when they could drive themselves wherever they wanted to go."

I won't miss the awkward interruptions in my own schedule, and I'm sure my wife won't miss the complications of arranging shared rides with other families (which she somehow has handled graciously and efficiently all these years). But I will certainly miss the conversations, because car time can be some of the best conversation time of all—if we nudge ourselves in that direction.

Seven Minutes and Counting

The author Sherry Turkle, who has done so much to help us realize the dangers to real relationship that come along with technology's promised benefits, suggests in her book *Reclaiming Conversation* that most conversations take at least seven minutes to really begin.[1] Up until that point, we are able to rely on our usual repertoire of topics—the weather, routine reports about our day, minimal and predictable chitchat. But around seven minutes, there is almost always a point where someone takes a risk—or could take a risk. The risk may be silence; it may be an unexpected question or observation; it may be an expression of a deeper or different emotion than we usually allow. All true conversations, really, are risks, exercises in improvisation where we have to listen and respond without knowing, fully, what is coming next, even out of our own mouths.

The tragedy of our omnipresent devices, Turkle suggests, is the way they prevent almost any conversation from

Stunted Conversations

My family does not know how to have a conversation anymore because we are all on our phones/devices.

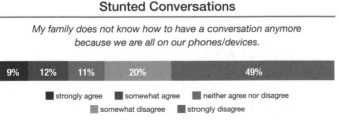

| 9% | 12% | 11% | 20% | 49% |

■ strongly agree ■ somewhat agree ■ neither agree nor disagree
■ somewhat disagree ■ strongly disagree

n = 1,021 US parents of children ages 4 to 17; due to rounding, the numbers do not add up to 100

unfolding in this way. A conversation interrupted several times before the seven-minute mark does not get deeper more slowly; it stays shallow, as each party makes room for the other to opt out and return to their device. What might be on the other side of the seven-minute mark, we never find out.

Car rides, for many of us in car-centric America, give us some of our best chances to break the seven-minute barrier. Ideally, the dinner table can serve this purpose as well, especially if dinner is our daily Sabbath hour away from distracting technology. But in the car, we're arguably even more present to one another, and physically closer to one another, than at the dinner table (and for many families, at least some nights of the week, schlepping from one activity to the next, the car *is* the dinner table!).

Auto Nirvana

But this is not how most of us treat the car ride. The next time you're the passenger in a car, start watching the people in cars you pass. Of course, the great majority in most places and times of day will be solo drivers. (An alarming number of them will be visibly preoccupied with their cell phones, an activity that impairs driving more than moderate alcohol consumption, but try not to be too freaked out by that.)[2] But watch for cars with someone in the front passenger seat. In

158

my informal observations, I find that a good 80 to 90 percent of them are obviously "on their phone," a phrase that used to mean making a voice call but now of course simply means engaged in some screen-based diversion. They are mere inches away from a fellow human being, probably a family member or friend, but despite that—or maybe because of that—they are mentally miles away.

And this starts earlier and earlier. The availability of in-car DVD players, as well as phones and tablets, allows harried parents to "bewitch" their children into compliant silence as they drive from place to place. We solve the immediate problem of how to keep small, squirmy children from going ballistic in the backseat, but we also teach our children, sometimes before they can talk, that the car is a place to be entertained, one more boring spot where, thanks to technology, you don't have to notice how bored you really are. We miss out on cultivating the virtue of patience, the kind of patience that can help us survive or even enjoy a long car ride (or a short one—I've seen parents who only had a mile to drive from the grocery store to home fire up the DVD player for their toddlers).

Honestly, I get it. When you're just trying to get the groceries home while they're still frozen, without dealing with a meltdown in the third row of the minivan, a little bewitched silence is close to heaven (or, more accurately, nirvana—the realm beyond all being where our earthly passions are extinguished). Who wants to turn every trip home from

The Disruption of Devices

Electronic devices are a significant disruption to our family meals.

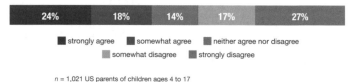

24%	18%	14%	17%	27%

■ strongly agree   ■ somewhat agree   ■ neither agree nor disagree
■ somewhat disagree   ■ strongly disagree

n = 1,021 US parents of children ages 4 to 17

the store into an opportunity to build character? Except, of course, that's exactly what character is made of—daily, slow, sometimes-painstaking steps toward handling everyday challenges with courage and grace. And these opportunities are not just for our children but for us too, figuring out how to cultivate our own patience and spark our own creativity as we deal with their sometimes unreasonable or impossible desires.

And creativity is definitely required. Young children don't generally engage in extended conversations about the meaning of life, and nothing can squelch a conversation with most teens like the sense that their parent is desperately trying to conjure up some "quality time." The great, deep conversations that are possible in the car after the seven-minute mark grow out of practicing simply staying engaged with each other and the world around us. With toddlers who are just becoming verbal, the best "conversation" is musical: making up simple, joyfully silly songs or rhymes that they can learn and echo over and over again. We had months of delightful car time when our children were learning the alphabet, just spotting letters as we drove along (our son, Timothy, gleefully called out every *t* in sight for several months). Later, we sequenced the alphabet, looking for each letter in turn on street signs (often stuck for miles on the letter *j*).

And we don't have to make up all the conversation on our own. The car is the perfect place for reading—for audiobooks that, unlike videos, can engage and involve the driver as well as the passengers, or for reading aloud to one another. During pauses in the reading, our conversations will be deeper and better, enriched by the way story enlarges our vocabulary and imagination. Back in the days of the iPod, during car trips our family designated the music player as the "wePod"—played through the car's sound system, not through individual earbuds. We've loosened that rule in recent years, but only after the pattern was set: we are here to share an experience together.

None of this comes automatically or easily, for children or parents. There will be childish meltdowns—on the part of children and parents. Something about the confined quarters and limited options of the car brings out the very worst in all of us at one time or another. Of course, that too is part of developing wisdom.

But those same confined quarters can also, if we persevere with patience and creativity, eventually bring out the best in

The majority of parents do not blame technology for a breakdown in family conversations. Less than one in ten parents (9%) say they strongly agree that their family does not know how to have a conversation anymore because they're all on their phones (or devices), only 12 percent somewhat agree, and an additional 11 percent are neutral. Half of parents (49%) strongly disagree with the statement and one-fifth (20%) somewhat disagree. When it comes to family meal time, parents are a little more apt to admit this space has been disrupted by electronic devices: one-quarter (24%) say they strongly agree that electronic devices are a significant disruption to their family meals, with an additional nearly one-fifth (18%) saying they somewhat agree.

us. One friend, now an adult, still drives every year with her parents from Colorado to Nevada the day after Christmas, even though she and her siblings are scattered around the country the rest of the time. "We have our best conversations on those drives," she tells me. "It's my favorite day of the year."

Most of us wouldn't sign up to turn our car rides into Dad's School of Wisdom and Virtue—unless there was something truly better waiting on the other side. So set the pattern early: car time is conversation time. We're on this trip together, and to make it to the end and gain wisdom and courage along the way, we're going to need to talk, for seven minutes and more.

Crouch Family
Reality Check

It is true that some of the best conversations we've ever had with our children, from very early in their lives right through the summers of their high school and college years, have been in the car. It's also true that one of my wife's great disappointments early in our marriage—she uses the very kind word *adjustments* instead—was discovering that when I am driving on long trips, I all too readily withdraw into silent absorption with the road, missing the chance to talk at length with the love of my life. I've tried to learn, in recent years, to make the most of the chance to talk with my wife as well as my kids, and we have had some seven-minute moments, and seventy-minute moments, where real insights and breakthroughs came.

And yes, when you pass our car on the highway on long trips to visit family, you may see some white earbuds in the ears of Crouch children (or spouses). You might even spot the two kids, now practically grown up, watching Pixar in the backseat. But you may also catch a glimpse of one of us reading aloud to the others, or our son gleefully explaining the history and structure of the music we're listening to as we drive, or the whole family pitching in on planning the meals for the next week, with our daughter and her love of fantastical cooking ideas taking the lead. And even if Dad is driving and tempted to withdraw, you might catch him listening, and talking too.

8

Naked and Unashamed

> **8. Spouses have one another's passwords, and parents have total access to children's devices.**

There is nothing in our society that has surrendered more completely, and more catastrophically, to technology's basic promise, easy everywhere, than sex.

For countless generations, sex was hardly ever easy, and it certainly was not everywhere. It was not *easy*, above all, because it was intimately connected to the begetting of children, and the arrival of a child is one of the most gloriously complicated events that can befall a human being. As far as possible from being *everywhere*, sex was meant to be confined to a single lifelong marital relationship, where—as almost any married couple can tell you—sex can be fulfilling and rewarding, but it is by no means always easy.

The one-flesh union of traditional marriage, as it was understood for centuries, united two biologically differentiated creatures who, while both image bearers of God, were almost always invested with profoundly different sexual capacities, desires, and needs. And the lifelong nature of that ideal union meant that marital sex did not just encompass the breathless, hormone-fueled days of early attraction but also long years of middle age and old age—all subject to the vicissitudes of each partner's health, each one's waxing and waning desires, and the thousand ups and downs that come with any lifelong relationship. Furthermore, many human beings would spend long seasons of their lives outside such a union, whether because of lack of a suitable partner, a call to priestly or monastic celibacy, or their husband's or wife's early death.

The sexual drive is among the most powerful sources of human behavior, so it is no surprise that even in the most traditional environments, the norms of marital sexuality and nonmarital chastity were bent and broken in countless ways. But the powerful social incentives to conform to the underlying norms, along with the ever-present likelihood of conceiving a child from male-female intercourse, meant that while there was probably always plenty of extramarital sex, it would never, ever have been described as easy everywhere.

In the span of one lifetime—my own, which conveniently enough began in 1968, the year that marked the apex of the social and sexual revolutions of the twentieth century—all these norms have been swept away. For most American youth and young adults, thanks to the relentless messaging of popular and mass culture, sex is indeed everywhere. This is true not only in the imaginative world of media but also in their actual experience, in relationships unsupervised by adults or extended family. Especially among young adults, but even among many middle schoolers and high schoolers, the easy-everywhereness of sex is dramatically increased by easy-everywhere access to alcohol, cannabis, or other drugs. They cast a haze of lowered inhibition over the inescapable vulnerability of sex, even for the most jaded and "experienced."

The norm, now, is for sex to be everywhere, available to everyone at every stage of life and in every configuration of desire, and to be easy—that is, unencumbered by consequences, hang-ups, or commitments. Marriage is now an entirely separate matter; it is not about the sexual union of two profoundly different expressions of human image bearing but fundamentally about a declaration of love by two people that is usually meant to include sexual exclusiveness but is by no means the exclusive domain for sex. Sex itself can and should happen, especially according to the dominant cultural messages, wherever there are willing and consenting participants—two, or more than two, or for that matter just one.

All this has been tremendously assisted by technology. Above all, technology has made contraception affordable, routine, nearly foolproof, and low maintenance. And medical treatments have rendered most sexually transmitted diseases (now simply and casually called "infections") manageable for most residents of the affluent Western world.

With sex dissociated so completely from the family, it is perhaps not surprising that family itself, so totally the opposite of easy-everywhere life, is being reconfigured. One in three children in the United States live without their biological father in the home.[1] And as family becomes less solid and stable, the parental oversight that used to guide and restrain youthful sexuality diminishes. Growing up without one's biological father, specifically, is related to everything from early onset of puberty, to early initiation of sexual activity, to vulnerability to sexual advances from nonbiologically related household members like stepfathers and half siblings.[2] Even those who grow up with both their mother and father are often plunged into the unsupervised environment of college at age eighteen, and on average they will not marry until their late twenties, if they marry at all.[3] Adrift in this chaotic and complex environment, young people have to sort out for themselves a vision of what sex is and should be.

And right there to help them acquire and manage a technology-saturated, easy-everywhere view of sex is the ultimate easy-everywhere sexual technology: pornography.

The New Normal

Streaming into our homes and onto our phones—accounting, by the most widely cited estimate, for 30 percent of all internet traffic—pornography provides and portrays a world where sex is easy.[4] Sex is widely available in porn. Almost everyone depicted is accessible and eager, and even the truly disturbing forms of porn that depict reluctance or resistance end with a dominating person getting exactly what he or she desires, sometimes through violence. Pornographic sex can be endlessly customized, so that it appeals perfectly to every possible set of desires and "needs." It purports to have no consequences except pleasure and an appetite for more of the same. It comes with no entanglements and is completely under the user's control (or so it seems—until porn users find themselves entangled in addiction to porn itself). And it certainly is everywhere—and not just in professionally produced or distributed forms but in a whole set of poses, postures, practices, and assumptions that are replicated in advertising, music videos, and ultimately in everyday behavior by teens and younger children who may not even know, at first, what they are imitating. The most prolific creators of pornography, in the sense of still and moving images designed to arouse, are not professional pornographers but ordinary people, starting in the teenage years. An astonishing 62 percent of teenagers say they have received a nude image on their phone, and 40 percent say they have sent one.[5]

The porn-saturated culture comes to see sex itself as a kind of technological enterprise—to be assisted with various devices and techniques that ensure satisfaction, remove vulnerability and uncertainty, and require neither wisdom nor courage, just knowledge and desire (and knowledge of one's own desires). The next frontier in porn will be enhanced by virtual reality and robotics, so that devices substitute entirely for other people, allowing for a perfectly controllable experience of solitary ecstasy.

It is all, of course, a lie. Evidence is piling up that the earlier and the more you use porn, the less you are capable of

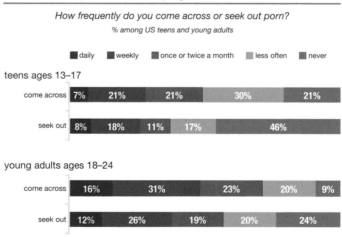

The Ubiquity of Porn

How frequently do you come across or seek out porn?

% among US teens and young adults

■ daily　■ weekly　■ once or twice a month　■ less often　■ never

teens ages 13–17

come across	7%	21%	21%	30%	21%
seek out	8%	18%	11%	17%	46%

young adults ages 18–24

come across	16%	31%	23%	20%	9%
seek out	12%	26%	19%	20%	24%

n = 813 US teens and young adults ages 13 to 24; July 2015; due to rounding, numbers may not add up to 100; © Josh McDowell Ministry

real intimacy with real partners.[6] There is no lasting sexual performance, let alone satisfaction, without the development of wisdom and courage—how could there be for something so core to human existence? There is no technological way to replace becoming the kind of people who know ourselves and know another well enough to truly, deeply give ourselves to them. But as with all addictions, by the time you discover the disappointing reality of pornified sex, you are very often unable to break free on your own. Technology's promise of shortcuts around the long path of wisdom and courage turns out to be a lie.

All of us would want to spare our children, our spouses, and ourselves from this plague, but in one sense, none of us can. If you have teenage children, whether boys or girls, it is likely that they have already been exposed to pornography and that they have sought it out. It is not just individuals who become addicted to porn; our whole society has embraced the underlying easy-everywhere view of sex that feeds it. And yet there are both nudges and disciplines we can embrace that will give us a fighting chance of real faithfulness and intimacy—and ultimately, real family. And they begin, not with any direct assault on porn itself, but with everything that we have covered so far in this book.

All addictions feed on, and are strengthened by, emptiness. When our lives are empty of relationships, porn's relationship-free vision of sex rushes in to fill the void. When our lives are empty of meaning, porn dangles before us a sense of purpose and possibility. When our lives have few deep satisfactions, porn at least promises pleasure and release. Nearly half of teenagers who use porn, according to Barna's research, say they do so out of boredom—higher than for any other age group (see the chart "Reasons Teens Search for Porn").

So the best defense against porn, for every member of our family, is a full life—the kind of life that technology cannot provide on its own. This is why the most important things we will do to prevent porn from taking over our own lives

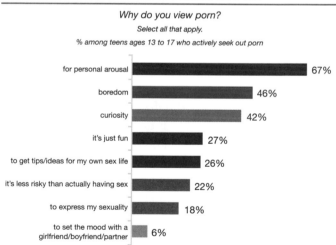

Reasons Teens Search for Porn

Why do you view porn?

Select all that apply.

% among teens ages 13 to 17 who actively seek out porn

for personal arousal	67%
boredom	46%
curiosity	42%
it's just fun	27%
to get tips/ideas for my own sex life	26%
it's less risky than actually having sex	22%
to express my sexuality	18%
to set the mood with a girlfriend/boyfriend/partner	6%

n = 543 US teens ages 13 to 17 who actively seek out porn; July 2015; © Josh McDowell Ministry

and our children's lives have nothing to do with sex. A home where wisdom and courage come first; where our central spaces are full of satisfying, demanding opportunities for creativity; where we have regular breaks from technology and opportunities for deep rest and refreshment (where devices "sleep" somewhere other than our bedrooms and where both adults and children experience the satisfactions of learning in thick, embodied ways rather than thin, technological ways); where we've learned to manage boredom and where even our car trips are occasions for deep and meaningful conversation—this is the kind of home that can equip all of us with an immune system strong enough to resist pornography's foolishness.

That is part of why this chapter comes toward the end of the book rather than at the beginning, even though almost every parent's number one concern about technology is the risk of exposing children to pornography and other forms of accelerated sexuality. The truth is that if we build our family's technological life around trying to keep porn out, we will fail. Pornography saturates our society even if you somehow manage to never click on an "NSFW" (not safe for work) website. When I was a child there was a popular television drama called *The Boy in the Plastic Bubble*, featuring an impossibly young John Travolta, about a boy suffering from an immune disorder, confined by his parents and doctors to a germ-free plastic enclosure. The drama, of course, centered on his constant quest to escape. The path to health is not encasing our children in some kind of germ-free sterile environment that they will inevitably try to flee; rather, it is having healthy immune systems that equip us to resist and reject things that do not lead to health. Everything up to this point in the book has been about creating that kind of healthy immune system for everyone in our homes—becoming the kind of people who see technology's shallow pleasures for what they are and set their sights on pursuing something better and deeper, together.

The Naked Truth

That being said, even people who have healthy immune systems do well to put on rubber gloves, if not a hazmat suit, when they deal with especially toxic environments. And there are some things we can do to minimize our exposure to the toxicity of pornography.

The most basic internet equivalent of gloves and safety goggles, of course, is a good filter. Internet technology changes rapidly enough that a book like this isn't the best guide, and no system will provide foolproof protection, but parents who do not implement powerful filters on the data streaming into their home are foolish about both their children's vulnerability and their own. (Our home internet is filtered by the OpenDNS service, which constantly updates and blocks sources of sexually explicit content as well as other objectionable material.) We also waited until our children were nearly at the end of high school to provide them phones with independent data plans that could circumvent our home internet. It is astonishing how many parents blithely give young children smartphones that allow absolutely unfettered access to whatever the internet (and links from their friends) may serve up.

The truth, though, is that any automatic system for blocking unwanted content is a leaky sieve at best (and no match for a savvy and determined teenager). We need something more powerful: accountability, transparency, and visibility, all in the context of relationship.

So my friend Matt, who has four middle- and high-school-age sons, has told each one, "I'm your dad. Until you are grown, it's my job to know more about what's going on in your life—and therefore on your phone—than anyone else." His sons know that he can, and will, look over their shoulder at any moment, and that he can, and will, and does, pick up their phone without needing to ask and browse through their messages and apps and history.

To many parents, and to nearly every American teenager, this will seem like an impossible invasion of "privacy." But Matt's sons have plenty of privacy. He doesn't barge into their bedrooms, and he can't, and wouldn't want to, police their secret thoughts or their conversations with friends at school. He makes a great deal of room for his sons to come

175

The Loneliness of Trying to Quit Porn

Do you have anyone in your life who is helping you avoid pornography?

% among US teens and young adults who would like to stop using porn

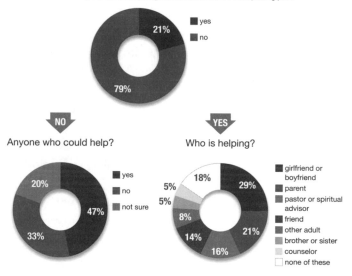

n = 351 US teens and young adults who say they want to stop using porn; July 2015; © Josh McDowell Ministry

to their own conclusions about their convictions and to develop, or not, their inner spiritual and emotional lives. What Matt understands, though, is that if mature adults struggle to handle the pipeline of temptation, titillation, and distraction that comes with 24/7 access to the internet, there is no way still-developing teenagers can handle it. His oversight is strictest where the technology is most powerful and potentially out of control.

And when you spend time with Matt, his wife, Kim, and their boys—and with his sons' friends, who flock to him because of his infectious sense of humor, his relentless respect for kids, his willingness to ask and answer any question, his warmth as well as his strictness, and perhaps above all his endless humility and openness about his own struggles and failures from his high school years to the present—you realize he's the kind of dad every child is dying to know.

So the tech-wise family will make a simple commitment to one another: no technological secrets, and no place to hide them. If your family has a shared computer, arrange it so the screen faces the rest of the room and others who may wander in. Until children reach adulthood, parents should have total access to their children's devices. I'm well aware this won't stop teenagers from deleting text messages the moment they arrive, relying on self-destructing apps like Snapchat, and engaging in countless other subterfuges—if they choose. But when they do so, they will know they are violating a family practice of openness to and with one another; they will be making choices, even poor ones, within a moral framework rather than simply blundering their way through adolescence without any guidance or boundaries.

Likewise, spouses should have one another's passwords and should cultivate the complete freedom to ask one another anything at any time. Even more than parents and children, spouses are bound for life as "one flesh." This level of access is not a matter of managing, let alone preventing, failure and sin. It has a simpler and deeper purpose: to keep us deeply connected to one another in ways that make failure and sin both less attractive and less damaging to our souls and our relationship. All sin begins with separation—hiding from our fellow human beings and our Creator, even if, at first, we simply hide in the "privacy" of our own thoughts, fears, and fantasies. Anything that short-circuits our separation, that reinforces our connection to one another and our need for one another, also cuts off the energy supply for cherishing and cultivating patterns of sin.

Will we avoid the technological maelstrom of easy-everywhere pseudosex (since that is all it is, nothing like the real, far more complex and beautiful, God-given thing) by keeping our filters up, sharing our passwords, and monitoring our children's devices? Hardly, any more than residents of the most polluted cities in the world can purchase enough air filters to avoid ever breathing in noxious fumes and dangerously tiny particles. But we can limit the damage it does to ourselves, our marriages, and our children. To use an older and hilariously apt metaphor attributed to Martin Luther, we can't stop the birds from flying over our head, but we can stop them from building a nest in our hair.

We rob the easy-everywhere world of its power to seduce us not so much by the rules we put in place as by the

The rise of digital pornography and its effects are hard to overstate. More than half of teens seek out pornography (only 46% say they "never seek it out") and the numbers are much higher for young adults ages 18 to 24 (less than one-quarter of whom never seek it out). Even when they aren't actively seeking it out, teens and young adults regularly come across it (only 21% of teens and 9% of young adults say they never come across porn). While most teens say they seek out porn for personal arousal (67%), substantial minorities regularly view porn out of boredom (46%) and curiosity (42%). With such significant access (whether they want it or not), adult discipleship in this area is critical. Yet the vast majority of teens (79%) say they have no one in their life helping them avoid pornography. And those who do are most likely to say it's a girlfriend or boyfriend rather than a parent or spiritual advisor.

dependence on one another we cultivate—depending on one another to help us be our best selves, growing in wisdom and courage and serving one another, in a world that wants to make us into shallow slaves of the self. Among the most heartening findings in the largely horrifying research on pornography use and addiction is that even people who plunge into addiction can emerge from that shallow madness, retrain and rewire their brains, and rediscover real intimacy.[7]

It takes time and trust, but it can be done. Lifting one another out of the tombs of addiction, slowly unwrapping the grave clothes, and calling one another back to life—as well as nudging and urging one another toward the life that really is life—that is what family is for.

Reality Check

It's painful to admit that, beyond the basic filtering of our home internet service, we haven't had the same level of courage and involvement that our friends Matt and Kim have in their children's lives. We've talked many times with our kids about the distortions of our pseudosex-obsessed world—enough, we hope, to give them healthy immune systems for all they will encounter and have already encountered. But there is probably more we don't know than is really healthy about our family's exposure to porn.

And I have had to confess to Catherine my own failures. I will never forget coming home from a dinner party at one of the residence halls of Harvard, where we lived and worked at the time, knowing that I had to tell Catherine the truth about my enmeshment in pornography. Telling the searing truth about my foolishness was a brutal contrast to the urbane conversation earlier in the evening. But as painful as it was, it was one of the most enduringly fruitful moments of my life. Her dismay and her forgiveness were the two essential ingredients in freeing me from my enslavement to porn's unreality—probably because it is only the combination of dismay and forgiveness that keeps any of us sane.

What Matters Most ③

9

....

Why Singing Matters

9. We learn to sing together, rather than letting recorded and amplified music take over our lives and worship.

Once upon a time, we knew how to sing.

It's true in American life generally. When I was a boy, the national anthem was sung at baseball games and patriotic events by the entire assembled crowd. It wasn't sung *well*, necessarily—that high note on "rocket's red *glare*" was often pretty disheveled—but it was at least attempted.

Now, I can't remember the last time I was in a public place where the whole crowd had the job of singing the national anthem. Instead, we've assigned that job to experts, professional or aspiring singers who sing on our behalf (sometimes badly, but still boldly). The rest of us simply do what we are going to do for the rest of the game: watch, listen, and enjoy as someone else demonstrates skill and courage.

This is also true in American Christianity. We once knew how to sing. Many great renewal movements within Christianity have been linked with a renewal of communal singing. (Even some of the not-so-great renewal movements, the ones that ended up in heretical dead ends like the Shakers, were still noted for their magnificent songs.) The founder of Methodism, John Wesley, began to question and deepen his own faith when he heard German Moravians singing during a terrible storm on board a ship bound for the United States.[1]

There are still places in American life where you can hear amazing singing welling up from an entire gathered community, not just from a professional chorus or choir. Almost all of them are in church. But even in church, those places and moments are fewer and fewer. In my travels around the United States, I'm in many different kinds of churches and worship environments. I've also studied singing and worked as a professional musician, not least in historically black churches that have kept gospel music and the tradition of Negro spirituals alive, and I know something of what human beings are capable of doing with their voices. In most places I go, the singing is a faint echo of what would be possible from the people assembled if they were asked, let alone trained, to sing.

Not that our churches are without music. Our worship bands are more technically proficient than ever, and louder than ever. The people holding microphones are singing, often expertly and almost always passionately. It's just the rest of us who, like the crowd at a ballgame, are mostly swaying along, maybe echoing a few of the phrases or words.

At the root of the disappearance of shared singing in public life and our churches is one of the most profound changes in the history of human beings, who have made music, as far as we can tell, from the very beginning. Up until about one hundred years ago, there was only one meaning to the phrase "play music." It meant that someone had to take up an instrument, having developed at least some skill, and make music, in person, in real time. They were not always expert musicians—the diaries and novels of the nineteenth century are full of rueful comments about how poorly some cousin played the piano in the family parlor. But there was only one way for music to be "played"—and that was for someone to play it.

Today, to "play music" can mean something totally different. The glorious technological magic of recorded music is now absolutely ubiquitous around the world. With a few taps or clicks I can call up a lifetime's worth of music over the internet and play it through speakers or headphones—an astonishing abundance that is truly easy and everywhere. And in one sense, the quality of the music I can summon with my devices is far higher than anything ever heard in the days when playing music meant an actual embodied activity; indeed, many professional recordings, thanks to editing and engineering, are far better than the original performance ever was.

Like so much of technology, there is no way to deny that this easy-everywhere abundance of music is a gift. And it has also caused us to forget and neglect what every other generation of human beings, in every culture, remembered and cultivated: the ability to make music on our own. Sitting in the living room or on the porch singing together, or listening to one another play instruments, was once a normal part of many American families' lives together. Today, I dare say, for the vast majority of American families it would seem impossibly corny and embarrassing. We can consume more music than they ever did; we create less music than they ever could have imagined.

If this just affected our leisure lives, it would be sad but perhaps not tragic. At least no one has to put up with artless cousins playing the piano in the evening anymore. But the reorientation of our musical lives around consumption is robbing us of something deeper; it is robbing us of a fundamental form of worship.

Worship, Wisdom, and Courage

I said at the beginning of the book that the real purpose of family is to develop wisdom and courage—to give us a deep understanding of the world and an ability to act faithfully in that world. But we cannot develop wisdom and courage only inside the walls of our home. Every family that cares about wisdom and courage needs to be part of a community larger than itself—a community that takes us deeper in our understanding of the world's beauty and brokenness, and that calls us to greater character than we would ever muster on our own.

The Christian conviction is that the best such community is the church: the true family of which all of our smaller families are merely partial signs. And the most distinctive thing the church does—the thing that most directly develops wisdom and courage in us, from childhood through old age—is call us to worship the God who made us in his image.

Worship is the path to true wisdom. "The fool says in his heart, 'There is no God'" (Ps. 14:1 NIV). And since human beings cannot actually live without some sort of god—some sort of ultimate reality—the fool makes something else god, often himself. But this leads to a shallow and dangerous view of the world. Worship brings us to the real truth about the world, its original intention and its ultimate meaning, and our responsibility in it. And this is not just a matter of merely knowing that truth; we must respond with our whole being to that truth and the One who is the source of that truth.

If you want to be wise, then, the most important thing you can learn to do is worship.

Worship is also the path to real courage. This might not be true if it were a merely informational activity, like taking a

Churchgoing among American Families

*When was the last time you attended a church service
other than for a holiday, wedding, or funeral?*

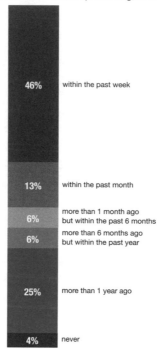

46% within the past week

13% within the past month

6% more than 1 month ago
but within the past 6 months

6% more than 6 months ago
but within the past year

25% more than 1 year ago

4% never

n = 1,021 US parents of children ages 4 to 17

weekly class on the Bible. Just because you know something is true doesn't mean you have the courage to act on it. But worship is actually more like a form of training—practicing, week after week, ideally in the presence of others who are further along in faith than we are, the exertion of our heart, mind, soul, and strength in the direction of giving glory to God. And Christians believe that God actually responds and moves in the midst of our worship: when we gather ourselves to offer him praise, he in turn dwells with us. At its best, worship transforms us, making us people capable of things we could never work up the capacity or courage for on our own: the ability to sacrifice, to love, to repent, to forgive, and to hope.

Worship reminds us of the shape of true life. One of the biggest threats to wisdom and virtue in a technological age is that we can so easily settle for something less than the best. What kind of life do we want for our children? The easy, safe, protected life afforded by modern technology—the kind of happiness that leisure and affluence can buy? Worship calls us out of the small pleasures of an easy-everywhere world to the real joy and burden of bearing the image of God in a world where nothing is easy, everything is broken, and yet redemption is possible. Think about the most beloved hymn in the English-speaking world, "Amazing Grace," and how deeply it embodies these themes—so much so that the rock star Bono and the American president Barack Obama have both led audiences in singing it. At the really crucial moments of greatest beauty and tragedy, only music that flows from the heart of the gospel is really enough.

And so worship is the most important thing a family can do. It is the most important thing to teach our children and the most important thing to rehearse throughout our lives. The Jewish people have known this ever since they were commissioned by God to be his chosen people. The central words of Israel's worship life are directly connected to family life:

> Hear, O Israel: The LORD is our God, the LORD alone. You shall love the LORD your God with all your heart, and with all your soul, and with all your might. Keep these words that I am commanding you today in your heart. Recite them to your children and talk about them when you are at home and when you are away, when you lie down and when you rise. Bind them as a sign on your hand, fix them as an emblem on your forehead, and write them on the doorposts of your house and on your gates. (Deut. 6:4–9)

Even today, observant Jewish families place these very words, written by hand on a small scroll of parchment, in a small case on the doorposts of their homes. The home is the place where worship of the true God starts: the place where we remember and recite God's Word, and where we learn to respond to God with our heart, soul, strength, and—as Jesus added when he called this the greatest commandment—with our mind as well.

And while it doesn't say so in this text, I believe the very best way to learn to worship, at home or in our churches, is to sing.

Worship is more than singing, of course. But there is something about singing that is fundamental to Jewish and Christian worship—starting with the Psalms, continuing with the hymns that grew out of the early church and the renewal and revival movements of subsequent centuries, finding new expression in the chants of Christian slaves in the American South, and abounding even today in a profusion of "worship music."

Simply, singing may be the one human activity that most perfectly combines heart, mind, soul, and strength. Almost everything else we do requires at least one of these fundamental human faculties: the heart, the seat of the emotion and the will; the mind, with which we explore and explain the world; the soul, the heart of human dignity and personhood; and strength, our bodies' ability to bring about change in the world. But singing (and maybe only singing) combines them all. When we sing in worship, our minds are engaged with the text and what it says about us and God, our hearts are moved and express a range of emotions, our bodily strength is required, and—if we sing with "soul"—we reach down into the depths of our beings to do justice to the joy and heartbreak of human life.

To sing well—not in the sense of singing in perfect tune or like a professional, but in this sense of bringing heart, mind, soul, and strength to our singing—is to touch the deepest truths about the world. It is to know wisdom. And it's also to develop the courage and character to declare that God is this good, that we are this in need of him, that we are this thankful, that we are this committed to be part of his story.

In too many of our churches, however, we have settled for a technological substitute for worship: amplification, which allows a few experts to do the worshiping on our behalf while we offer far too little of our own heart, soul, mind, and strength. As a working musician I do appreciate what amplification makes possible. In many ways, amplification is to sound what a cathedral is to space, creating a sense of wonder and transcendence out of ordinary stuff. The best amplification actually undergirds and calls forth great singing from the whole assembly.

But too often, instead, amplified voices and instruments let the rest of us off the hook; overwhelm our voices, which could be so powerful but instead sound by comparison so feeble; and subtly teach us that those of us without microphones are just consumers of worship rather than active offerers of it.

Rehearsing for Glory

It is absolutely possible to learn to really sing. You may or may not be able to learn to sing on pitch, but you can learn to sing with heart, mind, soul, and strength. The best time to begin to learn is in childhood, when our brains are primed for learning, our neuromuscular system is most able to be trained to connect mind with strength, and we are fearlessly willing to try something new. And of all the components of well-led worship, singing is the one that is most immediately accessible and engaging to children (listening to sermons takes a while longer!).

So the tech-wise family will do everything in their power to involve their children from the earliest possible age in expressions of church that model this kind of worship—not just the pleasant ditties of Sunday school or "children's church" but the full-throated praise that can come from people of every generation gathered in the presence of God. Maybe that isn't the Sunday-to-Sunday reality where you worship (it's only sometimes so in our own church), but it's worth exposing our children to the communities and places that have kept alive the powerful tradition of Christian song.

And as much as possible, we'll sing at home, when friends and family gather, as we clean up the kitchen and fold the laundry, as we celebrate holidays like Christmas and Easter, when we get up in the morning and when we lullaby ourselves to sleep. Our singing will be nothing like the auto-tuned, technologically massaged pop music that provides the bland sound track for the consumer life; it will be the sort of singing you only can do at home, where you are fully known and fully able to be yourself. And it will be a rehearsal for the end of the whole story, when all speech will be song and the whole cosmos will be filled with worship.

On January 12, 2010, a massive and devastating earthquake struck just outside Port-au-Prince, the capital city of Haiti. Countless buildings in the city collapsed and over a hundred thousand lives were lost. The already shaky electric

Over recent years, Barna research has shown a decline in regular church attendance among Americans. Still, nearly half of parents say they've attended a church service in the past week (46%), and an additional 13 percent say they've attended in the past month. Only 4 percent say they have never attended church, but a sizable one-quarter of parents say it's been more than a year since they attended a church service other than for a holiday, wedding, or funeral.

power grid was effectively destroyed, along with every other form of infrastructure. That night, with aftershocks rolling through the ground, almost all the residents of the city and the surrounding countryside stayed outside, torn with grief and fear. The residents of the poorest nation in the Western Hemisphere had little access to the easy-everywhere life of technology even before the earthquake, and now, with their world in ruins, they had none.

And they sang. When you don't have technology, you still have song. When you've lost everything, in fact, you still have song.[2]

All over the hills of Haiti those first terrible nights, under the starlit sky, the voices of the people of Haiti rose up in grief and lament, in prayer and hope.

They had something we have almost lost—and they still have it, as anyone who has visited a Haitian church or family knows. We can have it in our homes, and in our churches too, if we choose not to let technology do the singing for us.

. . . . Crouch Family . . . .
Reality Check

There are many things we've done poorly, belatedly, or distractedly in our family, but one thing I am most grateful we have done intentionally is sing together. As with many of our best efforts at intentional life, we have done best at this one during certain seasons of the year—especially Advent and Christmas, when we take advantage of the almost inexhaustible supply of magnificently singable Christmas carols.

And we are grateful that our church keeps the amplification to a reasonable level. In recent years we've been attending a smaller service in a chapel that was the original church building, built one hundred years ago and designed for singing. The service is sparsely attended and formal in a way that young people are supposed to find boring. But in fact our teenagers love it, partly because everything depends on the congregation's singing. Somehow, in that small service, where some members of the congregation are too old to sing with full voice, our kids can grasp more easily that they matter to the life of the church—that worship won't happen unless all the generations show up with their heart, mind, soul, and strength.

10

··

In Sickness and in Health

10. We show up in person for the big events of life. We learn how to be human by being fully present at our moments of greatest vulnerability. We hope to die in one another's arms.

Early in our marriage, Catherine and I made a commitment that has in turn dictated a hundred other decisions over the years. We decided that every time we were invited to a wedding or a funeral, unless circumstances made it truly impossible, at least one of us would go. We would cancel or reschedule anything else we had planned, and spend any money we had, to be present in person.

The value of commitments like this is they make decision making easier. When wedding invitations have arrived over the years, or we have learned of someone's death and the family's desire to have us there for their funeral, we haven't had to decide whether to go. The question is simply how. Though there have been a few times when it was, to our great regret, impossible for us to travel, this already-made decision has served us well over and over and given us some of the most memorable and transformative experiences of our lives.

One of the great gifts of technology is the simulation of presence at a distance. Starting with the telephone (which literally means "distant speech"), and continuing in recent years with Skype and FaceTime, we have been able to communicate, with higher and higher fidelity, with people far away. Now that our son is in college, thirteen hundred miles from home, we have a weekly video call as a family that has brought some of the best conversations we have had in his whole life—at no cost beyond the devices and services we already have.

Of course, much of the distance between us and people we love is itself the result of technology. It is partly because of air travel that we can imagine sending our children thousands of miles away from home in the first place; we can move away from our parents for a new job, or simply a more exciting location, knowing that we can visit them with a relatively easy car or plane trip. Technology, which does so much to close the distance, also enables much of the distance in our lives.

But even the highest quality Skype connection is not enough for the really important moments in a human life. You can think of it purely in terms of information, which can be measured as a stream of digital bits. A high-definition video call transmits something like 1.2 megabits per second[1] and can provide amazingly clear sound and images of the person we are talking with. But when we are present in person with another human being, our bodies are probably taking in and absorbing many gigabits per second—a thousand times more information. This information is not just in the form of sight and sound, both far richer and more subtle in person than even the highest quality connection can provide, but potentially comes through all the other primary senses as well: touch and smell and even taste. And almost certainly our bodies sense another person's presence in ways that we are not even aware of, let alone able to record or transmit. Any sort of mediated presence is the palest shadow of what it is like to be with another person in person—that is, present in the fullness of what our bodies make possible.

This is why Catherine and I decided that being present, in person, at the moments in human life that are truly unique and unrepeatable was worth any sacrifice of time or money. Only by showing up in person can we feel and grasp the full weight, joy, and vulnerability of the most important experiences in human life.

Showing Up

So the last, best commitment we can make in our mediated world is to show up, especially for the moments when we are most deeply human—which is to say, most deeply connected to our bodies. In old wedding vows the groom would say, as he put the ring on his bride's finger, "With my body I thee worship." A Christian wedding unites two bodies in such a way that they become not "one soul" but "one flesh." Although many couples cherish the video recordings of their wedding, no one should aspire to be married by video. Showing up in person at a wedding, even just as a guest, is a way of honoring that bodily commitment, just as showing up in person at a funeral is a way of honoring the fullness of the one we loved. And these public moments are so significant because they correspond to even more profoundly intimate bodily realities. Though these invitations are rarer, for good reasons, there is nothing so holy as to be present for a birth—or for a death.

When we show up, especially in the course of family life, we encounter what technology tries so hard to delay or erase: the limits and fragility of our bodies.

Our families care for us as infants, when our bodies are impossibly small and fragile and incapable, at first, of even the simplest self-care. They see us wail with distress as well as laugh in delight. They hold us close in those first weeks and smell perhaps the most amazing aroma in all of human experience, the fragrance of a newborn child—or they smell some of the most noxious odors a human body can produce.

Our parents see us in the gangly awkwardness of adolescence, and adolescents see their own parents subtly softening (and often fattening!) into middle age.

We see one another, at all ages, laid low by fever, noses running with colds, or bent over the toilet in nausea—and these are just the most common and unremarkable sicknesses. Our families also see us in far graver circumstances—coming home from what was meant to be a routine exam with a terrifying diagnosis; recovering from life-saving but physically devastating surgery; reeling from sudden and permanent change from accident or war or violence; descending gradually but unmistakably into confusion and dementia, no longer able even to recognize the ones we have most loved.

And our families see us, and we see them, in the final passage of life. I believe it was the author Wendell Berry who made the devastating observation that in every family that gathers around the Thanksgiving dinner table, one member will one day be left entirely alone, having buried all the others. We bind ourselves to one another with all our love and loyalty, but one day all those bonds will be severed by loss.

If there is anything we would do with technology if we could, it would be to cheat death. Indeed, our modern science and all the technology it provides us emerged in no small part from exactly that quest—the alchemists' search for the philosopher's stone, the substance that would turn other metals to gold and give mortals immortality.

And indeed, in all kinds of ways technology has given many of us, for long seasons of life, something close to easy-everywhere health—antibiotics that almost magically halt the invasion of bacteria, anesthesia that makes possible procedures that would have been inconceivable before, even various ways to stave off the most obvious forms and signs of aging. But this very success has reawakened the alchemists' old dream: discovering a way of manipulating the world that would save us from ever having to die.

The actual result of a technological pursuit of everlasting life will be, for many who attempt it, a life that is ultimately not worth living: ending one's days not at home in the care of family but in the purposely sterile, impersonal, technology-stuffed environment of a hospital, at incredible expense, enduring ever more invasive "heroic" measures until we finally expire. Alarmingly, there is evidence from research that the people most likely to request these futile but fantastically expensive final measures are actually Christians—the very ones who should be most able to trust their mortal bodies to the care of God.[2] Something has gone wrong when atheists and secular people are more able to face the inevitable reality of death than the people who should believe that death has been conquered and does not have to be feared.

The tech-wise family will choose a different way. We will recognize that our daily bodily vulnerabilities, our illnesses, and our final journey to death are our best chance to reject technology's easy-everywhere promise. We will embrace something better: the wisdom of knowing our own limits, the courage to care for one another, and, just as difficult, the courage to accept one another's care when we cannot care for ourselves. We will put love into practice in the most profound possible way, by being present with one another in person at the greatest and most difficult moments of life.

For one thing we can say for sure is that when we are at our body's very limits, nothing but personal presence will do. A few years ago I had the great gift of being invited into the bedroom of my friend David Sacks, born in 1968 just like me but brought to the end of his life by cancer that, by the time it was discovered, had erupted throughout his body. After a glorious and grace-filled year of life made possible by medical treatment, David's illness outran the drugs. In his last days he lay on his bed. The body that once had effortlessly beaten me in game after game of squash was now unbearably thin and weak. David was an internationally celebrated photographer, but he would never make another image. He had sent me countless text messages over the years—I never will have the heart to delete them from my phone—but now he was beyond text messaging. He had created a Facebook group where he and his wife, Angie, chronicled the story of his cancer diagnosis, treatment, and all the ups and downs that followed, but he would never again update it.

But he was still there, still with us, still able, just barely, to hear us praying and singing—able, in moments of lucidity, to open his eyes, take in the small group of family and friends gathered around his bed, and know he was not alone. His brother brought a guitar and we sang, several nights in a row, Matt Redman's song "10,000 Reasons."

The technology was over. The easy-everywhere dream had ended. Now we could only be here, in our own vulnerable bodies, present to the immensely hard reality of a friend, father, son, and husband dying. Over the bed was a framed, calligraphed rendering of David and Angie's wedding vows.

It was one of the hardest places I have ever been. It was one of the most holy places I have ever been. It was one of the best places I have ever been.

Homeward

We are meant to build this kind of life together: the kind of life that, at the end, is completely dependent upon one another; the kind of life that ultimately transcends, and does not need, the easy solutions of technology because it is caught up in something more true and more lasting than any alchemy our technological world can invent. We are meant to be family—not just marriages bound by vows and the children that come from them, but a wider family that invites others into our lives and even to the threshold of our very last breath, to experience vulnerability and grace, sorrow and hope, singing our way homeward. We are meant not just for thin, virtual connections but for visceral, real connections to one another in this fleeting, temporary, and infinitely beautiful and worthwhile life. We are meant to die in one another's arms, surrounded by prayer and song, knowing beyond knowing that we are loved.

We are meant for so much more than technology can ever give us—above all, for the wisdom and courage that it will never give us. We are meant to spur one another along on the way to a better life, the life that really is life.

Why not begin living that life, together, now?

Acknowledgments

Thank you to Roxanne Stone and David Kinnaman of the Barna Research Group. I'm grateful to you for your research-based honesty about the world we live in and your faith-based hope for life in the midst of it. Thank you as well to Chaz Russo for the fantastic infographics design. And deep thanks to Kathy Helmers and the team at Creative Trust for your consistently perceptive and faithful counsel in the work of writing.

One of the great gifts of my life has been the chance to meet some of my heroes. Among them is the philosopher who first illuminated technology for me, and whose work has indelibly shaped this book—and our family's life. When I did finally meet him, Albert Borgmann was every bit as wise and courageous as I could have hoped. It was especially delightful that we met in the blissfully cell-phone-free Frio River canyon, thanks to the hospitality of Laity Lodge. Thanks to Steven Purcell and to the conveners of that meeting, David Wood and Arthur Paul Boers, for providing such a rich environment for going deeper into the best things.

I'm grateful for the many, many friends who have shared the joys, quandaries, and calamities of parenting and family life with us. Among so many I could name, this book especially benefited from conversations with, and simply life with, Elizabeth and Karl, Matt and Kim, Jill and Andy, Caleb and Kathy, and Angie. We love and admire and have learned so much from you.

Most of all, thank you to Catherine, who discovered my excessive fondness for technology early on and has responded with such patient sanity to it (and me) ever since. And to Timothy and Amy—unwitting but willing participants in our fitful family journey toward wisdom and courage—may your lives be far, far better than easy everywhere.

For Further Reading

If I were to suggest one book to take up after this one (if not before it), it would be Sherry Turkle's *Reclaiming Conversation: The Power of Talk in a Digital Age* (Penguin, 2015). John Dyer's *From the Garden to the City: The Redeeming and Corrupting Power of Technology* (Kregel, 2011) is an especially wide-ranging and readable assessment of technology from a specifically Christian perspective. From the Fuller Youth Institute team, *Right Click: Parenting Your Teenager in a Digital Media World* (by Art Bamford, Kara Powell, and Brad Griffin; Fuller Youth Institute, 2015) is a practical, levelheaded guide to life with teenagers in the age of connected devices.

This book is most influenced by the life work of Albert Borgmann, especially his 1987 book *Technology and the Character of Contemporary Life: A Philosophical Inquiry*

(University of Chicago Press). Dr. Borgmann's work is, entirely appropriately, far from light reading, so you may want to warm up with one book that influenced him and has delighted and directed our own family: Robert Farrar Capon's *The Supper of the Lamb* (Modern Library, 2002; first published 1970). Though it was published nearly fifty years ago, Capon's theological cookbook is still the ideal summons to something better than our technological shallows—in the kitchen and everywhere else. *Bon appétit*—and *bon courage*.

Notes

Introduction: Help!

1. Nancy Sleeth, *Almost Amish: One Woman's Quest for a Slower, Simpler, More Sustainable Life* (Carol Stream, IL: Tyndale House, 2012).

2. Richard H. Thaler and Cass R. Sunstein, *Nudge: Improving Decisions about Health, Wealth, and Happiness* (New Haven: Yale University Press, 2008).

3. See, for instance, Catherine de Lange, "No Pain, No Gain? Getting the Most out of Exercise," *Guardian*, January 13, 2014, https://www.the guardian.com/science/2014/jan/13/no-pain-no-gain-exercise-heart-health -dementia-cancer.

4. Dietrich Bonhoeffer, *Life Together*, trans. John W. Doberstein (New York: Harper & Row, 1954), 77.

Chapter 1 Choosing Character

1. "Bisphenol A (BPA)," National Institute of Environmental Health Sciences, last reviewed July 15, 2015, http://www.niehs.nih.gov/health/topics /agents/sya-bpa/index.cfm.

2. "Contraceptive Use in the United States," Guttmacher Institute, September 2016, https://www.guttmacher.org/fact-sheet/contraceptive-use -united-states.

3. G. K. Chesterton, *Charles Dickens*, in *The Collected Works of G. K. Chesterton*, vol. 15, *Chesterton on Dickens* (San Francisco: Ignatius, 1989), 188.

4. Jonathan Vespa, Jamie M. Lewis, and Rose M. Kreider, "America's Families and Living Arrangements: 2012," United States Census Bureau, August 2013, https://www.census.gov/prod/2013pubs/p20-570.pdf.

Chapter 3 Structuring Time

1. Dan Lyons, *Disrupted: My Misadventure in the Start-Up Bubble* (New York: Hachette, 2016).

2. Dan Lyons, "Congratulations! You've Been Fired," *New York Times*, April 9, 2016, http://www.nytimes.com/2016/04/10/opinion/sunday/congrat ulations-youve-been-fired.html?_r=0.

3. Albert Borgmann, *Technology and the Character of Contemporary Life: A Philosophical Inquiry* (Chicago: University of Chicago Press, 1984), 136–37.

4. William Alden and Sydne Ember, "Banks Ease Hours for Junior Staff, but Workload Stays Same," Dealbook, *New York Times*, April 9, 2014, http://dealbook.nytimes.com/2014/04/09/banks-ease-hours-for-junior-staff -but-workload-stays-same/?_r=0.

5. Andy Crouch, *Playing God: Redeeming the Gift of Power* (Downers Grove, IL: InterVarsity, 2013), chap. 13.

Chapter 4 Waking and Sleeping

1. "Sleep, Learning, and Memory," Division of Sleep Medicine at Harvard Medical School, last reviewed December 18, 2007, http://healthysleep .med.harvard.edu/healthy/matters/benefits-of-sleep/learning-memory.

2. Jessica Schmerler, "Q&A: Why Is Blue Light before Bedtime Bad for Sleep?," *Scientific American*, September 2, 2015, https://www.scientific american.com/article/q-a-why-is-blue-light-before-bedtime-bad-for-sleep/.

3. Barna Group, survey of 1,021 US parents of children ages four to seventeen, January 25 to February 4, 2016; see "About the Research" for more information.

Chapter 5 Learning and Working

1. Ferris Jabr, "The Reading Brain in the Digital Age: The Science of Paper versus Screens," *Scientific American*, April 11, 2013, https://www .scientificamerican.com/article/reading-paper-screens/.

2. See, e.g., Marily Oppezzo and Daniel L. Schwartz, "Give Your Ideas Some Legs: The Positive Effect of Walking on Creative Thinking," *Journal of Experimental Psychology: Learning Memory, and Cognition* 40, no. 4 (July 2014): 1142–52.

3. See, e.g., Connie Kasari et al., "iPads Can Help Children Learn Spoken Language: FAQ & Tips from Experts," Autism Speaks, https://www.autismspeaks.org/family-services/technology/iPad-FAQ-Tips.

Chapter 6 The Good News about Boredom

1. *Oxford English Dictionary*, 2nd ed., s.v. "bore"; *Merriam-Webster Dictionary*, online ed., s.v. "ennui," accessed October 18, 2016, http://www.merriam-webster.com/dictionary/ennui.

2. *Oxford English Dictionary*, 2nd ed., s.v. "bore."

3. "Lawns and Lawn History," The Lawn Institute, accessed October 18, 2016, http://www.thelawninstitute.org/pages/education/lawn-history/lawns-and-lawn-history/.

4. J. R. R. Tolkien, *The Lord of the Rings* (Boston: Houghton Mifflin, 1994), 32.

5. Sally Lloyd-Jones, *The Jesus Storybook Bible: Every Story Whispers His Name* (Grand Rapids: Zonderkidz, 2007).

Chapter 7 The Deep End of the (Car) Pool

1. Sherry Turkle, *Reclaiming Conversation: The Power of Talk in a Digital Age* (New York: Penguin, 2015), 153, 322.

2. Ralph Hanson, "Text Messaging Deemed More Dangerous Than Alcohol or Cannabis behind the Wheel," Motor Authority, September 18, 2008, http://www.motorauthority.com/news/1029714_text-messaging-deemed-more-dangerous-than-alcohol-or-cannabis-behind-the-wheel.

Chapter 8 Naked and Unashamed

1. Jonathan Vespa, Jamie M. Lewis, and Rose M. Kreider, "America's Families and Living Arrangements: 2012," United States Census Bureau, August 2013, https://www.census.gov/prod/2013pubs/p20-570.pdf.

2. One good summary of the extensive literature on father absence is *Father Facts 7* (Germantown, MD: National Fatherhood Initiative, 2016).

3. D'Vera Cohn et al., "Barely Half of U.S. Adults Are Married—A Record Low," Pew Research Center, December 14, 2011, http://www.pew socialtrends.org/2011/12/14/barely-half-of-u-s-adults-are-married-a -record-low/.

4. Sebastian Anthony, "Just How Big Are Porn Sites?," Extreme Tech, April 4, 2012, http://www.extremetech.com/computing/123929-just-how -big-are-porn-sites.

5. Barna Group, *The Porn Phenomenon: The Impact of Pornography in the Digital Age* (Ventura, CA: Barna, 2016), 28–29.

6. A recent example is Chyng Sun et al., "Pornography and the Male Sexual Script: An Analysis of Consumption and Sexual Relations," *Archives of Sexual Behavior* 45 (May 2016): 983–94.

7. A good introduction from a Christian point of view to the neuroscience of pornography—for men—is William Struthers, *Wired for Intimacy: How Pornography Hijacks the Male Brain* (Downers Grove, IL: InterVarsity, 2010).

Chapter 9 Why Singing Matters

1. "The Moravians and John Wesley," *Christianity Today*, accessed October 18, 2016, http://www.christianitytoday.com/history/issues/issue -1/moravians-and-john-wesley.html.

2. I heard of the widespread singing in Haiti from friends who were there at the time of the earthquake, and its extent is similarly attested in Elizabeth McAlister, "Soundscapes of Disaster and Humanitarianism: Survival Singing, Relief Telethons, and the Haiti Earthquake," *Small Axe: A Caribbean Platform for Criticism* 39 (November 2012): 22–38.

Chapter 10 In Sickness and in Health

1. Polycom, Inc., *Preparing Your IP Network for High Definition Video Conferencing*, accessed October 18, 2016, pg. 3, http://www.polycom.com /content/dam/polycom/common/documents/whitepapers/hd-video-con ferencing-wp-enus.pdf.

2. Andrea C. Phelps et al., "Association between Religious Coping and Use of Intensive Life-Prolonging Care near Death among Patients with Advanced Cancer," *Journal of the American Medical Association* 301, no. 11 (March 18, 2009): 1140–47.

About the Research

We live in a complex, rapidly changing world, and such times require guides to help us navigate. Data can serve as such a guide, especially when paired with the insight and wisdom of trusted leaders such as Andy Crouch.

In partnership with Andy, Barna Group conducted a public opinion survey among 1,021 US parents, nationally representative of parents with children ages 4–17 who live in their home at least 50 percent of the time. In addition to this survey, you'll find statistics from four other Barna Group studies referenced in *The Tech-Wise Family*. You can find the survey methodology for all five of these surveys below.

All of the research studies identified below, with the exception of the research on pornography, were independently funded by Barna Group. The pornography research was conducted on behalf of Josh McDowell Ministry (a CRU Ministry).

Once data was collected, minimal statistical weights were applied to several demographic variables to more closely correspond to known national averages.

When researchers describe the accuracy of survey results, they usually provide the estimated amount of "sampling error." This refers to the degree of possible inaccuracy that could be attributed to interviewing a group of people that is not completely representative of the population from which they were drawn. For the general population surveys, see the table below for maximum sampling error.

There is a range of other errors that can influence survey results (e.g., biased question wording, question sequencing, inaccurate recording of responses, inaccurate data tabulation), errors whose influence on the findings cannot be statistically estimated. Barna makes every effort to overcome these possible errors at every stage of research.

As with all self-reported data, it is important to note the responses for the parent study are self-reported responses by parents (who also report for their children) and thus are based on perceptions and recall rather than diary or other tracking of actual behaviors.

The varying generations of parents naturally have children in various ages/stages. Millennials tend to have children who are preschool or in lower grades; generation Xers' and boomers' children are typically older—in middle school or high school. As a result, activities and use of technology may differ due to the stage their family is in.

Survey Methodology and Sampling Error

Dates	Participant demographics	Collection method	Sample size	Sampling error
January 25–February 4, 2016	US parents (of children ages 4–17)	online	1,021	± 2.9
July 20–23, 2015	US teens and young adults ages 13–24	online	813	± 3.4
February 3–11, 2015	US adults	online	1,000	± 3.1
June 25–July 1, 2013	US adults	online	1,404	± 2.4
May 9–20, 2013	US adults	online	1,086	± 2.8

About Barna Group

Barna Group is a research firm dedicated to providing actionable insights on faith and culture, with a particular focus on the Christian church. Since 1984 Barna Group has conducted more than one million interviews in the course of hundreds of studies and has become a go-to source for people who want to better understand a complex and changing world from a faith perspective.

Barna's clients include a broad range of academic institutions, churches, nonprofits, and businesses, such as Alpha, the Templeton Foundation, Pepperdine University, Fuller Theological Seminary, the Bill and Melinda Gates Foundation, the Maclellan Foundation, DreamWorks Animation, Focus Features, Habitat for Humanity, the Navigators, NBCUniversal, the ONE Campaign, Paramount

Pictures, the Salvation Army, Walden Media, Sony, and World Vision.

The firm's studies are frequently quoted by major media outlets such as BBC, CNN, Fox News, the *Economist*, *USA Today*, the *Wall Street Journal*, the *Huffington Post*, the *Atlantic*, the *New York Times*, and the *Los Angeles Times*.

About the Author

Andy Crouch—author, speaker, musician, and dad—has shaped the way our generation sees culture, creativity, and the gospel. In addition to his books *Culture Making*, *Playing God*, and *Strong and Weak*, his work has been featured in *Time*, the *Wall Street Journal*, the *New York Times*, and Lecrae's 2014 single "Non-Fiction." He was executive editor of *Christianity Today* from 2012 to 2016 and is now senior strategist for communication at the John Templeton Foundation. He lives with his family in Pennsylvania.